TRISTAN

a play by

Don Nigro

SAMUEL FRENCH, INC.

45 West 25th Street   7623 Sunset Boulevard
NEW YORK 10010   HOLLYWOOD 90046
LONDON   *TORONTO*

Copyright © 2003 by Don Nigro

ALL RIGHTS RESERVED

CAUTION: Professionals and amateurs are hereby warned that TRISTAN is subject to a royalty. It is fully protected under the copyright laws of the United States of America, the British Commonwealth, including Canada, and all other countries of the Copyright Union. All rights, including professional, amateur, motion pictures, recitation, lecturing, public reading, radio broadcasting, television, and the rights of translation into foreign languages are strictly reserved. In its present form the play is dedicated to the reading public only.

The amateur live stage performance rights to TRISTAN are controlled exclusively by Samuel French, Inc. and royalty arrangements and licenses must be secured well in advance of presentation. PLEASE NOTE that amateur royalty fees are set upon application in accordance with your producing circumstances. When applying for a royalty quotation and license please give us the number of performances intended, dates of production, your seating capacity and admission fee. Royalties are payable one week before the opening performance of the play to Samuel French, Inc., at 45 West 25th Street, New York, NY 10010; or at 7623 Sunset Blvd., Hollywood, CA 90046, or to Samuel French (Canada), Ltd., 100 Lombard Street, Lower Level, Toronto, Ontario, Canada M5C 1M3.

Royalty of the required amount must be paid whether the play is presented for charity or gain and whether or not admission is charged.

Stock royalty quoted on application to Samuel French, Inc.

For all rights other than those stipulated above, apply to Samuel French, Inc.

Particular emphasis is laid on the question of amateur or professional readings, permission and terms for which must be secured in writing from Samuel French, Inc.

Copying from this book in whole or in part is strictly forbidden by law, and the right of performance is not transferable.

Whenever the play is produced the following notice must appear on all programs, printing and advertising for the play: "Produced by special arrangement with Samuel French, Inc."

Due authorship credit must be given on all programs, printing and advertising for the play.

ISBN 0 573 62952 8   Printed in U.S.A   #22268

No one shall commit or authorize any act or omission by which the copyright of, or the right to copyright, this play may be impaired.

No one shall make any changes in this play for the purpose of production.

Publication of this play does not imply availability for performance. Both amateurs and professionals considering a production are *strongly* advised in their own interests to apply to Samuel French, Inc., for written permission before starting rehearsals, advertising, or booking a theatre.

No part of this book may be reproduced, stored in a retrieval system, or transmitted in any form, by any means, now known or yet to be invented, including mechanical, electronic, photocopying, recording, videotaping, or otherwise, without the prior written permission of the publisher.

IMPORTANT BILLING AND CREDIT REQUIREMENTS

All producers of TRISTAN *must* give credit to the Author of the Play in all programs distributed in connection with performances of the Play and in all instances in which the title of the Play appears for purposes of advertising, publicizing or otherwise exploiting the Play and/or a production. The name of the Author *must* appear on a separate line on which no other name appears, immediately following the title, and *must* appear in size of type not less than fifty percent the size of the title type.

CHARACTERS

Matthew Armitage (37)
Sarah Pritchard (17)
Rhys Rose (17)
Alison Morgan (19)
Gavin Rose (41)
Bel Rose (40)

SETTING

The Pendragon house in Armitage, Ohio, 1887-88, the law office in town, and other locations as follows: the desk of Matt Armitage in the law office in town is DR; the porch of the Pendragon house, with swing, RC; between the porch and the sofa in the parlor, C, is the entrance to the house, and just inside it steps leading up to a bedroom URC; upstage of the sofa is a wooden cabinet with liquor; the kitchen, represented very simply by a table with chairs, is LC; characters can move into other parts of the house by going upstage into darkness under the bedroom area UC and ULC; DL are some tombstones and just upstage of them a path leading off DL to the pond; upstage of the path is a bench under a large old tree L which is mostly out of view; the path leads past the tree up to the Indian caves ULC, on roughly the same level as the bedroom. All locations are present simultaneously and players should have very easy access from one location to another. The scene outside the dance should be played DC with the rest of the stage in dark shadows. All times and places interpenetrate so that transitions are instantaneous and persons from various times and places may be onstage, visible and in character at the same moment. The play must develop very fluidly with no stops, no blackouts, no actor ever forced to scuttle around in the dark out of character to rush into place for the next scene—either the actor has come on in character in the natural course of events, or has never left in the first place. Sometimes when a character in one location is speaking about another, we will be watching the person he's talking about. We are seeing the interconnected labyrinth of memories and experience of six people.

ACT I

Scene 1

(Night. Sound of an approaching thunderstorm. Lights up slowly on the desk in the law office in Armitage. Sound of a ticking clock. MATT ARMITAGE, a lawyer in his late thirties, sits at his desk, drinking whisky, and speaks.)

MATT. Storm brewing again. This is the rainy country and I am the king. Cato records somewhere that he only made love to his wife when it thundered. He also says he was glad when it thundered. I drink when it storms. I also drink when it doesn't storm, but I never get drunk. I try, but I fail. My grandfather was a drunkard. My father never drank at all. I drink like the former but remain as sober as the latter. *(Thunder. He drinks.)* It was in such a storm that she came to the Pendragon house one night, rain whipping around the corners, leaves smashing into the side of her face, the house making creaking and groaning noises like the rickety bed of desperate lovers, violent streams of water pouring off the roofs where gutters and spouts had rotted and broken. He found her standing at the foot of the porch steps, soaked and lovely, like a lost mermaid, and full of some private grief he could not then fathom. She knew the house when she saw it, though she'd never been there before. When he came down the steps she retreated through the broken trelliswork and under the porch where his mother's stray cats went to give birth. They could see one another in flashes of lightning. He couldn't persuade her to come out, so finally, now thoroughly soaked himself, he yanked her from beneath the house and carried her up the steps and through the door. It was all like a dream she'd had. She knew what to do. Don't be afraid, he said. But there was, in fact, as it turned out, much to fear.

(A flash of lightning and a great thunderclap. MATT drinks. The light in his office goes out.)

Scene 2

(Violent thunderstorm. Lights up on the Pendragon house. SARAH, a young housekeeper, moves from the kitchen into the parlor.)

SARAH. Rhys? Are we leaving the front door wide open now? What are you trying to do? Make a lake in the parlor? *(RHYS enters from the porch, carrying ALISON, who is struggling and screaming.)* What in the name of God—can't you even close the door behind you?

(SARAH disappears for a moment to close the door. The sound of the storm lessens. Alison has gotten her legs on the floor now but is still struggling with RHYS.)

RHYS. It's all right. You're safe here. Nobody's going to hurt you.

(He lets her go. ALISON looks around, holding her arms, uncertain what to do now.)

SARAH. *(Returning and looking at them.)* What the hell is that?
RHYS. What's it look like? It's a girl.
SARAH. It looks like a girl. What have you done to her? *(To*

ALISON.) What's he done to you?

(ALISON backs away from SARAH, turns and abruptly buries her face in RHYS's chest.)

RHYS. I haven't done anything to her.

SARAH. Is she bleeding?

RHYS. No, that's my blood. When I dragged her out from under the porch she got scared and bit me. It was an accident.

SARAH. Nobody bites anybody by accident. What was she doing under the porch? Having kittens?

RHYS. Hiding from me, I guess.

SARAH. You were playing hide and seek with a wild girl in a thunderstorm and she ran under the porch, and when you pulled her out she accidentally bit you, so you dragged her in the house, is that about it?

RHYS. That's close enough.

SARAH. Well, let go of her, why don't you?

RHYS. She doesn't seem to want to let go.

SARAH. A minute ago she was screaming bloody murder and trying to get away, and now she's on you like a barnacle. Is the girl daft?

RHYS. Maybe she just doesn't like you. Go and get some blankets, she's going to shiver herself to death. And don't rouse Mother.

SARAH. Rhys, if you're going to be abducting strange, wet girls that bite and dragging them into the house, I think your mother's going to notice sooner or later. She's not blind. She's insane, but she's not blind.

RHYS. Just get the blankets, all right?

SARAH. And don't order me around like some kind of servant.

RHYS. You are a servant.

SARAH. I just work here. This is temporary.

RHYS. Sarah, you've been here your whole life.

SARAH. Well, life is temporary.

RHYS. Look, I don't want to have a philosophical discussion right now, just go get some blankets.

SARAH. She's dripping all over the place. Your mother isn't going to like that one bit. And guess who's got to clean it up? Not you. You've never cleaned up a mess in your life. All right, I'm going, I'm going.

(SARAH disappears into the house, muttering darkly to herself.)

RHYS. *(Looking down at ALISON, who is still clutching him.)* You can let go. It's really all right. Do you want to sit down on the sofa? *(She won't let go.)* All right. We'll both sit down. *(RHYS moves crabwise to the sofa, ALISON still clutched onto him, and plunks himself down, ALISON ending up on his lap.)* Uhhhh. There. I was tired, anyway. Is that better? You're kind of a hard girl to figure out. First you won't let me near you, and now you won't let go. Is this what I should expect from women in general, or is this atypical behavior? I'm trying to learn these things as I go along, but so far I've just had Sarah and Mother to study up close, and they're pretty confusing. Sarah gets cranky when it storms, but she's actually very sweet. My mother, on the other hand, is more or less certifiable, but she can be nice, too, now and then. The girls in town are mostly either stuck-up prudes or kind of loose and silly, or some combination of the above. So what kind of girl are you? *(ALISON snuggles up with her head under his chin.)* What ever kind you are, you feel good. And you don't have to be afraid any more, whatever it is. I promise.

(Thunder. They hold each other more tightly. GAVIN comes down the steps.)

GAVIN. Rhys? What's going on down here? *(He stops, looks at ALISON.)* Who is that?

RHYS. I don't know. I found her out in the rain.

TRISTAN

GAVIN. What was she doing out in the rain?

RHYS. Looking at the house.

GAVIN. *(Pulling the hair gently back from ALISON's face so he can get a better look at her.)* It's all right. I'm not going to—

(ALISON looks at him. Pause.)

RHYS. What is it? Do you know her?

GAVIN. I don't think so.

RHYS. For a second there you looked like you recognized her.

GAVIN. Just for a moment I thought I did. But I was mistaken. *(He looks at ALISON.)* Are you all right?

RHYS. She hasn't said anything yet.

GAVIN. She can't talk?

RHYS. I don't know. She can scream.

GAVIN. Why are you bleeding?

RHYS. I had to drag her from under the porch and she bit me. She was afraid. She's fine now.

GAVIN. Do you have a name? I'm Gavin Rose, and this is my son, Rhys. Nobody here is going to hurt you.

BEL. *(Coming down the steps in her nightgown.)* Gavin, where the hell did you run off to? I was just starting to get warmed up.

GAVIN. Except maybe her.

BEL. Is this some sort of party? Why wasn't I invited? What the hell is that? It's a girl. And she's wet. Is she dead?

RHYS. No, she's not dead, Mama.

BEL. Well, why do you have a wet girl on the sofa? Did you fish her out of the pond?

GAVIN. He found her out in the storm.

BEL. Rhys, you really shouldn't bring things into the house like that. You don't know where they've been. Why are you bleeding? Did she bite you?

RHYS. Yes, she bit me. She was scared.

BEL. She looks like a drowned rat. But with breasts. Whose little discard are you, honey? I don't want any strays in my house.

GAVIN. As I recall, Bel, you've dragged every sort of lost creature imaginable into this house at one time or another.

BEL. It's one thing to bring in dumb animals, but people we should leave outside where they belong. Especially people who bite. Now, Rhys, you just take that girl back where you found her and leave her there. Maybe whoever lost her will come back and get her.

RHYS. I'm not taking her anywhere.

GAVIN. Bel, why don't you get us some blankets?

BEL. I'm not getting you blankets.

RHYS. Sarah's getting blankets.

GAVIN. You're both shivering. I'll get you some wine.

BEL. Don't give them wine. Why are you giving them wine?

GAVIN. Because they're cold.

SARAH. *(Returning with blankets.)* Here's your blankets. Oh, everybody's up now. This should be fun.

RHYS. What took you so long?

SARAH. I put some tea on.

GAVIN. I'm getting them wine.

BEL. Why do we need blankets?

SARAH. *(Putting blankets around RHYS and ALISON.)* They're wet, Mrs. Rose.

BEL. Why did you bring wet blankets?

GAVIN. Rhys and this girl are wet, Bel.

BEL. I know they're wet. I said they're wet, didn't I? Wasn't that me?

GAVIN. There's only one wine glass. What happened to the wine glasses?

SARAH. Mrs. Rose threw them at the preacher, the last time he came by.

GAVIN. Bel, you shouldn't throw things at the preacher.

BEL. Oh, he likes it. He keeps coming back, doesn't he? I'm just trying to cure his constipation. Besides, he looks like a toad.

GAVIN. *(Handing a full wine glass to RHYS.)* Try some wine.

BEL. Don't give my son wine. It'll rot his brain. Look what it did to me.

RHYS. *(Coaxing ALISON to drink.)* Here. Drink some of this. It's good. See? *(RHYS drinks a sip, offers the glass to her again. After a moment's hesitation ALISON takes the glass in both hands and drinks it down like water.)* Hey. Leave some for me.

SARAH. Well, we know she can drink. Does she have a name?

RHYS. She won't tell us.

ALISON. Alison. My name is Alison.

GAVIN. Alison what?

ALISON. I'm not sure.

BEL. She looks familiar. Where have I seen that girl before?

SARAH. Maybe on a wanted poster. She's been biting people all over the country.

GAVIN. Alison, do you know where you are?

ALISON. Not exactly.

GAVIN. This is the Pendragon house, in Armitage, Ohio. You'll be safe here. We'll take care of you.

BEL. Yes, you say that now, but before long you'll get bored with her and then I'll be the one who'll have to feed her and give her baths and clean her litter box.

GAVIN. Sarah, why don't you take Alison upstairs and find her something dry to put on? She's about Bel's size, I think.

BEL. You're giving her my clothes?

GAVIN. We're letting her borrow some just for now.

BEL. This is a catastrophe.

SARAH. *(Trying to pull ALISON up.)* Come on, then, girl. Come on. She won't let go of Rhys.

GAVIN. Rhys, go along with them.

BEL. You want her to change clothes with Rhys?

GAVIN. I want him to go along so Sarah can get her upstairs.

RHYS. *(Getting up, ALISON still clinging to him.)* I'll come with you, Alison. Mama's got some nice things you can wear.

BEL. I don't want her in my clothes. What if she's got fleas?

SARAH. *(Helping ALISON up the steps with RHYS.)* And don't you even think about biting me, girl. I bite back.

RHYS. It's true. I've got the scars to prove it.

(SARAH, RHYS and ALISON disappear up the steps.)

BEL. Gavin, doesn't that girl look familiar to you?

GAVIN. She looks lost.

BEL. She looks like the other one.

GAVIN. What other one?

BEL. The one that killed your father.

GAVIN. That was twenty years ago. This girl wasn't even born then.

BEL. That woman was a witch. She can do anything.

GAVIN. Just don't let your imagination run wild on you again.

BEL. Don't talk to me about my imagination. I have no imagination. I used to have one, but then I got better, and it went away, and since then I've been doing really well. Haven't I been doing well? Several days of the week I'm almost normal.

GAVIN. You've been doing extremely well, and I'm very proud of you, so don't spoil it now by getting all worked up over nothing.

BEL. But what if it's the curse, come back to kill us?

GAVIN. It's not a curse, it's just a girl.

BEL. It's that witch woman, come back in a younger body to destroy us and take the house. Don't look at me like I'm crazy. I've progressed way past crazy, towards an almost perfect illusion of sanity. I've developed a unique capacity to counterfeit self-possession. I had a child who wasn't a group of small pigs. I only have hallucinations when I'm sitting in the closet. So I think you owe it to me to take that girl by the neck and throw her out the window on her head.

GAVIN. I'm not throwing her out on her head. She's just some poor, lost girl who got caught in the rain, and she's a little confused. God knows, you should understand about being confused. Maybe this is a test. If you can handle this, it'll prove you're finally more or less sane. If you can be nice to this girl, if you can resist those intermittent demented impulses of yours, you'll know you've finally conquered your madness.

BEL. You think so?

GAVIN. Yes. I do. Do you think you can be nice to her?

BEL. I could if I wanted to. I've always fancied having a daughter. Maybe I could dress her up in doll clothes.

GAVIN. First I think you should just try to make friends with her.

BEL. Well, maybe. All right. I can do that. I'll put aside my very strong premonition that behind that innocent mask lurks a maggotty-faced, ancient succubus, and I'll be nice to her.

GAVIN. Good. Thank you.

BEL. Can we keep her in the corn crib?

GAVIN. No.

BEL. All right. Just asking. Fine. Nice. Fine.

(GAVIN and BEL look at each other. BEL looks a little squirrelly. GAVIN drinks wine. Lights fade on them.)

Scene 3

(MATT ARMITAGE at his desk.)

MATT. I was sitting at this desk one morning in the autumn of the year 1887 when someone tapped on the window. I looked up, and there, framed under the arch of old backwards lettering that said Pendragon & Armitage, Attorneys at Law, was a young girl looking in at me, with Rhys and Sarah on either side of her. For a moment I couldn't breathe. I had feared that she was dead.

(RHYS, SARAH and ALISON come into the office.)

RHYS. Matt, I want you to meet someone. This is Alison. She's going to be staying with us. Alison, this is Matthew Armitage. His father was my grandfather's law partner.

ALISON. *(Giving MATT her hand.)* I'm very pleased to meet you, Mr. Armitage. What a nice, cozy old office you have.

SARAH. If you want some clothes, come on, then. We haven't got all day.

RHYS. Just a minute, Sarah.

SARAH. I haven't got a minute. I've things to do.

ALISON. Rhys has told me a great deal about you, Mr. Armitage. He admires you very much.

MATT. If he does, that's the first I've heard of it.

ALISON. You seem to have your bags packed. I hope you're not leaving town, when I've just met you.

MATT. I was just about to catch a train to Maryland. I got word that a friend passed away, and I need to go and make some arrangements for the family.

SARAH. Can we get a move on, please? Let the man catch his train.

ALISON. Sarah's anxious to buy me some new clothes so I won't have to wear hers. I seem to have lost mine somewhere, and Mr. Rose has been nice enough to take me in. Don't you think that was kind of him, Mr. Armitage?

MATT. He's a kind man.

ALISON. He certainly seems to be.

MATT. Where exactly are you from, Miss—?

RHYS. Alison isn't quite sure. She might have gotten a bump on the head somewhere.

ALISON. I seem to be having a little trouble figuring out exactly who I am.

RHYS. We're taking her over to Doc McGort's to make sure she's all right.

ALISON. I feel wonderful. I'm just a bit confused at the moment. Everyone's being so good to me.

SARAH. I'm leaving. If anybody wants to come, fine. If not, you can just stay here all day and rot in place.

ALISON. I'd better go along with Sarah now, or she's going to explode. It was very good to meet you, Mr. Armitage.

RHYS. You two go ahead. I want to talk to Matt.

ALISON. I hope you two aren't going to gossip about me. I hate gossip, don't you, Mr. Armitage?

MATT. I'm not much for gossip, myself.

ALISON. I knew you were somebody I could trust. I knew it the first time I set eyes on you. You just have that look about you. Well, see you later, I hope. I have a feeling you and I are going to be great friends. Come along, Sarah. Don't dawdle. Let's buy me some clothes.

(ALISON goes out.)

SARAH. I'm going to kill her. Can I kill her, Rhys? Please? Matt, you'll defend me if I kill her, won't you?

RHYS. Just go on after her. She has no idea where she's going. And watch she doesn't step out in front of something.

SARAH. Maybe I could push her under a wagon. I could make it look like an accident.

RHYS. Sarah—

SARAH. All right, all right, but I liked her a lot better when she didn't talk. First she won't say anything, and now I can't get her to shut up. I don't know. I just don't know.

(SARAH goes out.)

RHYS. God, Matt, isn't she beautiful?
MATT. Which one?
RHYS. It's the most amazing thing. She just wandered up to our

house in the rain last night. She says her name is Alison, but she can't seem to remember much else. Father said to bring her in to town, buy her some clothes and take her to Doc McGort to have her looked at.

MATT. And you have no idea who she is?

RHYS. No. I was hoping you might recognize her. You know pretty much everybody in the county.

MATT. Sounds like quite an interesting little mystery.

RHYS. She's the most incredible creature. She was terrified when I found her. She'll be very quiet, and then suddenly she lights up and she's the most charming person, very affectionate, funny, interested in everything and everybody, teasing Sarah, and then she gets quiet again. Sarah wanted to just drop her off at the Sheriff's office, but you know what a jackass he is, and Father said maybe she'd be better off if we just kept her for a while.

MATT. I'll look into it, if you'd like.

RHYS. Thank you, Matt. I appreciate it.

MATT. I'm your lawyer. That's what I'm for.

ALISON. *(Coming back in.)* Rhys, stop bothering poor Mr. Armitage and come help me pick out some dresses, will you? Sarah's having a conniption fit. You will come out and see us soon, won't you, Mr. Armitage?

MATT. You can count on that.

ALISON. I'll be looking forward to it. See you then.

(ALISON smiles, takes RHYS by the arm, and pulls him out. MATT stands there, gets a bottle, and pours himself a drink.)

Scene 4

(ALISON walks by the pond, evening. Bird sounds. MATT at his desk.)

MATT. All day my mind was full of her. Drink, as usual, was no help. What did she think she was doing? I didn't take the train to Maryland. *(He begins to move towards ALISON.)* Instead, in the evening I went out to the Pendragon house, and found her walking alone by the pond.

ALISON. Hello, Matt. I knew you'd come. Thank you for not telling.

MATT. What are you doing here?

ALISON. I've come home.

MATT. Do you know how worried your sister's been?

ALISON. She knew this is where I'd be.

MATT. How could you run off and leave her to deal with your mother's death all by herself?

ALISON. My sister is a very resourceful person. She'll do fine. When Mother died, I just got on a train and came. I promised her I would, and that's what I did.

MATT. What do you think you're going to accomplish here?

ALISON. I don't know. I like it here. At least, I think I do. The people more than the house, which is odd, because Mother always led me to believe the house would be wonderful and the people horrible, but it seems to me to be just the opposite. The house scares me, but I feel very close to the people, the town, the woods and the pond and everything. I feel like I belong here.

MATT. This is not where you belong right now.

ALISON. It's exactly where I belong. It's my home.

MATT. That's your mother talking, not you.

ALISON. My mother is gone. And I've come home. That's all there is to it. You won't tell them who I am, will you? I think Gavin knows, but he hasn't said anything. I thought the first thing he'd do might be to contact you and try and get you to take me back to Maryland, but he hasn't done that, has he?

MATT. I haven't spoken to him.

ALISON. I'm sure he knows. He recognized me the minute he saw me. I look like my mother.

MATT. Yes, you do. Very much.

ALISON. But he hasn't said. Why hasn't he said?

MATT. Gavin is a very private man, and most of his life he's preferred not to know things.

ALISON. But he does know.

MATT. Then he prefers not to say. You put me in a very awkward position here. Gavin has always supplied the money to support you and your mother and sister—

ALISON. To pay us, for taking care of the house in Maryland. Don't make it sound like charity.

MATT. But he made my father promise never to mention anything about you to him.

ALISON. Why would he do that?

MATT. Partly I think he didn't want to upset Bel. She's not a person you want to get upset. And he just didn't want to think about it any more. Your mother was pregnant with you when she left, and Bel had a serious breakdown after what happened here. So my father handled it all for Gavin, and when my father died, I took over, and all these years Gavin hasn't said two words to me about it.

ALISON. So for all he knows, you could be robbing him blind.

MATT. He knows I'm not robbing him. We keep very complete records. He's looked at the books. I'm sure he's aware of every time you had a doctor bill or anything else. We just don't talk about it. That's his way.

ALISON. So now that I've shown up here, you don't know whether to come right out and tell him it's me, or just keep your mouth shut like he told you to. How will he find out my mother's dead? Come across the funeral expenses in your damned account books?

MATT. That's entirely possible.

ALISON. I think that's a really sick way to live.

MATT. And how would you characterize what you're doing?

ALISON. What do you think I'm doing?

MATT. I don't know what you're doing. Do you?

ALISON. Do you want me to just come out and tell everybody, to make things easier for you? Because I don't particularly care to make things easy for you. If Gavin doesn't want to talk about it, then it seems to me I should do him the courtesy of not forcing the issue.

MATT. What you should do is go home.

ALISON. I AM home. *(Pause.)* You've always been a good friend to me. I always looked forward to you and your father coming to Maryland, to the books you'd bring me, to playing chess with you. And you were kind to my mother, even when she wasn't always very nice to you. I don't want to cause you any trouble, I really don't. But I'm not going back.

MATT. Then what are you going to do?

ALISON. I haven't decided yet. I want to get to know them a little better first. After all, they are my family.

MATT. Alison, I can't let you hurt these people. You know that.

ALISON. What do you think I'm going to do to them? Kill them? A sweet, innocent little creature like me?

MATT. I'm going to have to speak to Gavin about it.

ALISON. You're not going to tell him, Matt. You know you're not.

MATT. Why aren't I?

ALISON. Because you're in love with me.

MATT. What kind of thing is that to say?

ALISON. A true thing. I know you people like to avoid the truth as much as possible, but my mother taught me to look with a cold eye and see what's there, and the truth is, you've been in love with me for a long time.

MATT. I'm married.

ALISON. Exactly.

MATT. Just what is that supposed to mean?

ALISON. You won't tell because you're in love with me, and because Gavin doesn't want to know, and because he already knows, and because if you do, I'll tell your wife about us.

MATT. Tell her what about us?

ALISON. That you're in love with me and you've been sneaking off to Maryland to see me for some years now.

MATT. My wife knows I go to Maryland.

ALISON. Does she know why?

MATT. I have no secrets from my wife.

ALISON. You've got one.

MATT. I don't know what you're talking about.

ALISON. What about when you held me in the chapel behind the house?

MATT. You were upset because your mother was dying. You were crying. What was I supposed to do?

ALISON. You wanted me.

MATT. I was comforting a person I've known since she was a child.

ALISON. I am not a child, and you desired me at that moment.

MATT. I pitied you.

ALISON. And you wanted me. Can you stand there and deny it? You're a fairly honest man, for a lawyer, and you know it's true. So I don't think you're going to say anything to anybody about me, are you?

MATT. If you're under the impression I'm going to let you blackmail me over something that didn't even happen, you're very much mistaken.

ALISON. Please, Matt. I don't want to fight with you. I just want some time to get to know my family. Just give me a little time with them. I think maybe that's why Gavin hasn't said anything. He needs time, so we can get to know each other. You've got a family. You've got a wife and a little boy. Just let me know my family. I don't want to hurt anybody here. I swear I don't. Maybe it won't work out.

Maybe I'll just go away and never tell them, but I've got to spend some time with them first. Don't I have a right to do that?

MATT. I'm going to Maryland tomorrow, to help your sister take care of things there. Why don't you come with me?

ALISON. I've got things to do here.

MATT. Alison, it's your mother.

ALISON. I know it's my mother. I'm doing what my mother wanted.

MATT. That's what scares me.

ALISON. How about this: you go to Maryland for a few days and get everything settled there, make sure Holly's all right. Let me stay here and get to know my family. Just don't mention it to Gavin before you leave. Is that too much to ask? You'll be doing your job. Gavin will have some time to bring it up himself if he wants to. Then when you get back we'll talk. Will you just give me that?

MATT. You really should come with me.

ALISON. I'm not going with you.

(Pause.)

MATT. All right. I'll give you a few days. But when I get back here, we're going to deal with this. And there's something you and I have got to get straight right now. Nothing has ever happened between us, and nothing ever will. I have a wife and a child that I love very much, and there never was and never will be anything between you and me. Is that clear?

ALISON. I would never want to do anything to hurt you, Matt. Or your wife, or your little boy. You're a very good friend of mine. I know I can always count on you. It's really an enormous comfort to me knowing that whatever happens, I can always count on you. Thank you.

(She kisses him on the cheek, but it's not exactly an innocent kiss. He looks at her. Then he turns and goes. ALISON looks after him. Bird sounds.)

Scene 5

(SARAH is making bread in the kitchen, slamming things around, irritated.)

SARAH. Struts around this house like the Queen of England. Thinks she can order me about. Doesn't do a lick of work. Just who does she think she is? Ought to throw her back out in the rain and lock the door, if you ask me. But nobody asks me. Nobody ever asks me.

ALISON. *(Coming into the kitchen.)* Can I help you with that, Sarah?

SARAH. No.

ALISON. I know how to make bread.

SARAH. Then you can see I don't need any help.

ALISON. Why do you always avoid me?

SARAH. I don't avoid you. I haven't got time to avoid you. I've got work to do. Unlike some people around here.

ALISON. I offer to help, but you won't let me.

SARAH. If you want to help, stop bothering me.

ALISON. Sarah, why don't you like me?

SARAH. It's not my job to like you.

ALISON. Is it your job to hate me?

SARAH. There's got to be a better way for you to waste your precious time than worrying about what I think of you.

ALISON. It's not a very Christian thing to hate somebody you hardly know.

SARAH. Hate is a very Christian thing. Read your Bible.

ALISON. I've read my Bible, and it doesn't say anything about hate being Christian. It says the opposite.

SARAH. Clearly you've only been reading selected parts.

ALISON. What does that mean?

SARAH. It means it's dangerous to listen to what people say unless you're also watching what they do while they're saying it.

TRISTAN

ALISON. You're a rather clever person, aren't you?

SARAH. What business have I got being clever? I'm just a poor servant girl.

ALISON. How long have you been here?

SARAH. All my life. My mother was housekeeper here before me. I don't know how she stood it. Sometimes I get so furious at them. But she took it all in stride—Mr. Rose and his brooding, Mrs. Rose and her bouts of lunacy, and cranky old Aunt Margaret—you're lucky that one did you the favor of expiring before you arrived. She was a handful. And Rhys and I were a handful as well, I suppose, when we were children. My mother died two years ago—we wore her out, is what happened. And I took over.

ALISON. But you couldn't have been more than fifteen then.

SARAH. I don't see what that signifies. Somebody had to do it. Anyway, I won't be here much longer. I should have left when Mother died. I don't know why I didn't.

ALISON. Maybe you felt sorry for them.

SARAH. They don't need me to feel sorry for them. They can do that for themselves. Besides, they've got a big house and some money left in the bank, and they still own half the town. I'll be out of here just as soon as they can find somebody else stupid enough to come and live in this godforsaken place.

ALISON. I don't see why that should be a problem. It's lovely out here.

SARAH. In town, they think the house is haunted, and the mistress is crazy, and they tell darker stories than that.

ALISON. What kind of stories?

SARAH. Why are you bothering me with all these foolish questions? Why don't you go bother Rhys? I'm sure he'll be happy to tell you any sort of rubbish you want to hear. The two of you get along so famously together.

ALISON. Sarah, I hope you're not jealous.

SARAH. Jealous of what?

ALISON. Of Rhys and me.

SARAH. What have I got to be jealous about?

ALISON. Well, you two are good friends, aren't you? You grew up together.

SARAH. You forget, I'm just the servant girl.

ALISON. I think you're a great deal more than that.

SARAH. You don't know anything about it.

ALISON. I was hoping you and I could be friends.

SARAH. Why would you want to be friends with me? I'm just—

ALISON. Just a poor little servant girl, yes, I know, we've heard that sad lament quite enough, thank you, but it doesn't get my sympathy.

SARAH. Who asked for your damned sympathy? And what the hell would you know about being a servant?

ALISON. My mother was a servant once.

SARAH. Well, what do you want? An award?

ALISON. You really do hate me.

SARAH. I don't think anything about you, except that you mean extra clothes to wash, food to cook, dishes to rinse, you drive me berserk in the kitchen, and when Rhys is around you he acts like he's feebleminded.

ALISON. You're in love with Rhys.

SARAH. Now that has got to be the single most idiotic thing I've heard in my life. And that's saying quite a lot, living, as I do, with Mrs. Rose. You needn't worry about me, honey. I'm no competition for you in that area.

ALISON. What did you do? Play doctor together?

SARAH. What we played is none of your business.

ALISON. I didn't come here to be your enemy, Sarah.

SARAH. Why exactly DID you come here?

ALISON. I'll tell you what I'm going to do. I'm going to help you around the house from now on, whether you like it or not.

SARAH. I don't want your help. You'll just get in the way.

ALISON. Here. I'll break the beans.

SARAH. You just keep your hands off my beans.

(ALISON sits down and begins breaking beans.)

ALISON. You and I are going to be great friends in the end, Sarah. Really great friends, I think.//
SARAH. Don't hold your breath.

(SARAH turns and goes out. ALISON smiles and breaks beans. BEL comes down the steps, through the parlor, and into the kitchen.)

BEL. What do you think you're doing with those beans?//
ALISON. I'm helping Sarah. I don't mind. It gives me time to think.//
BEL. You think?//
ALISON. On occasion I do, yes.//
BEL. That's unusual in a person your age.//
ALISON. No it's not. Sarah thinks. She also works very hard.//
BEL. Yes, and she'll never let us forget it. I hate work, myself. I'd much rather have visions and play my organ.//
ALISON. You have visions?//
BEL. Now and then, when the moon's right, and the squirrels are looking in the windows.//
ALISON. What do you see?//
BEL. I'd tell you, but I'm making an enormous effort at the moment to be nice to you.//
ALISON. Is it that difficult?//
BEL. It's damn near impossible, largely because you are, physically and in other respects, more than a little reminiscent of a sorceress we used to know.//
ALISON. A sorceress? Really?//
BEL. Oh, she pretended to be a normal woman, but I knew from the beginning she was playing pinochle with the Devil. I know all about the Devil—my daddy was a preacher. He used to eat skunkweed and have visions under my organ. I inherited certain things from him—fortunately, not the clap, but some of his psychic

powers. And you look just like that woman. You're so much the spitting image of her, I got to force myself not to spit at you.

ALISON. As far as I know, I'm not in league with the Devil. I don't think I am, anyway.

BEL. But you wouldn't tell me if you were, now, would you?

ALISON. I might. Just to throw you off. But I don't know. I'm not very good at hypothetical situations.

BEL. Now, you see, that's my specialty. When I have trouble is where the hypothetical starts turning into the actual, because a lot of the time I can't really tell them apart too good. But I'm better than I used to be. I don't carry pigs around any more in a potato sack, and I don't see dead triplets on the piano. I think that's got to be considered an improvement, don't you?

ALISON. Probably.

BEL. My husband still believes in his heart that I'm crazy as a basket of rats, which is understandable considering my past average distance of removal from what he rather naively considers to be reality. But for his sake I have striven mightily, over the last twenty years, against this gift of lunacy I've been blessed with. He married me out of pity because I was insane and pregnant by somebody he murdered in the war and the sister of his dead best friend, and then I gave birth to dead hairy triplets with tails and they came back to haunt me so I started keeping baby pigs under the bed, and then things started to get a little peculiar, but after it became clear that he'd impregnated me with Rhys—well, with something—we didn't know it was going to be Rhys—it could have been anything, but Gavin sat me down and told me that from now on I was going to have to work very hard at being sane, for the sake of our child, and I have for the most part done remarkably well since then, but every time I look at you, my brain catches on fire and I can't help feeling in my heart that you've been sent here to slaughter us like a bunch of sheep.

ALISON. Sent here? Who would send me here?

BEL. I figure either the Devil or God. I'm developing a theory they're actually Siamese twins. Or maybe it was that witch woman we drove out of here after Gavin's father and stepmother drowned themselves in the pond.

ALISON. I haven't been sent here to kill anybody.

BEL. Then what the hell are you doing here?

ALISON. Right now I'm just breaking beans. Would you like me to make you some lemonade?

BEL. Only if you have lemons. You're not trying to lull me into a false sense of security so you can sneak into my room some night and drive an egg beater into my brain, are you?

ALISON. No. I would never use an egg beater.

BEL. Well, that's a relief. Oh, God.

ALISON. What?

BEL. I just had this terrible sensation of warmth start creeping over me. I fear it might be the beginning of some sort of mild affection for you. Either that, or the change of life is coming on early. No, no, I'm actually starting not to hate you so much. I must be insane.

ALISON. Do you like sugar in your lemonade?

BEL. No. Sugar is for the morally infirm. I take it straight.

ALISON. So do I.

BEL. This is very disturbing, this vague sense of kinship with a potential rival. Is that what sane people feel? Or is it yet another unexpected turn in the complex and twisted evolution of my dementia? And how can I tell which is which?

ALISON. Well, really, what difference does it make, as long as you're having a good time?

(They look at each other. ALISON smiles. BEL smiles back, a little uncertainly.)

Scene 6

(Night. The sound of owls. RHYS under the old tree at the back of the house.)

MATT. *(At his desk, as we see ALISON approaching RHYS.)* At the back of the Pendragon house, near the pond, there's an ancient tree which must have been old when Robert Rose and James Armitage settled this part of east Ohio at the time of the Revolution. Often, at night, when he couldn't sleep, Rhys would go out and sit under that tree and think about her.

ALISON. I saw you from my window. At first I thought you were a ghost.

RHYS. Well, there's plenty of them around here. You should go back inside. It's cold out.

ALISON. I'm warm enough. Is something wrong?

RHYS. I come out here when I can't sleep, or when Mother goes off the deep end, or Sarah's giving me a hard time.

ALISON. Does she do that often? Sarah, I mean.

RHYS. More lately than usual.

ALISON. I hope it's not because of me. I wouldn't want to be the cause of any trouble between you and Sarah.

RHYS. It's just how we communicate with each other. We grew up together.

ALISON. Yes, I know. You played doctor.

RHYS. Sarah told you that?

ALISON. Not exactly. You know she's in love with you, don't you?

RHYS. Sarah? That's silly.

ALISON. It's not silly at all. It's true.

RHYS. Sarah is not in love with me. We've been at war more or less since we were children. Sarah is my friend.

ALISON. So you don't love her?

RHYS. Of course I love her. She's like the bad-tempered sister I never wanted but got anyway. Did you come out here in the middle of the night to talk about Sarah?

ALISON. I was just curious.

RHYS. About Sarah and me playing doctor?

ALISON. About all of you. About who you are. I mean, four people living in such a huge old house, mostly cut off from the rest of the town—it interests me. And you've been so nice to me. I just—I don't know. It's really pretty creepy out here at night, isn't it?

RHYS. Maybe we should go back inside and get some sleep before you catch cold.

ALISON. I don't want to sleep. I've been having bad dreams.

RHYS. About what?

ALISON. Don't laugh.

RHYS. I won't laugh. I promise.

ALISON. You swear?

RHYS. Cross my heart. What do you dream about?

ALISON. Dragons. I've been dreaming about dragons. You promised not to laugh. It's horrible. They look at me through the window with their big, red, bloodshot eyes, and breathe fire. Then somebody comes, a knight of some sort, looking rather like you, actually, and he cuts off the dragon's head. And the dragon is bleeding there, and the head is looking up at me, accusing me, as if it was all my fault, somehow. And then I wake up feeling like something horrible is going to happen. Do you think that means something?

RHYS. It means you should stop eating Sarah's rhubarb pie before you go to bed.

ALISON. I knew you'd make fun of me.

RHYS. I wouldn't worry about it. It's just a dream.

ALISON. I know it is, and ordinarily very little scares me, but dreams really bother me sometimes, I think because I can't control them. I need to feel like I'm in control of my destiny, but lately I haven't been feeling like that at all. Well, in the daytime, maybe, but at night, anything could happen. Also, I hate sleeping alone. When I was a little girl I always slept with my sister Holly. She took care of me.

RHYS. Alison, you remembered.

ALISON. Remembered what?

RHYS. You remembered your sister's name.

ALISON. I did?

RHYS. You just said it. You said her name was Holly, and you slept with her when you were a little girl. What else do you remember?

ALISON. I don't know.

RHYS. What about your parents? Do you remember your mother?

ALISON. My mother is dead.

RHYS. What about your father?

ALISON. I'm starting to get cold now. I think I'll go back inside.

RHYS. Alison?

ALISON. What?

RHYS. If you have bad dreams, you can always come and knock on my door. I'm just down the hall from you.

ALISON. I know where you are. But I don't think that would be altogether proper, would it? Me creeping into your room late at night. That could very easily turn into a—misunderstood situation.

RHYS. Could it?

ALISON. Yes. It could. Very easily. *(They look at each other. He kisses her. She pulls away.)* I don't think you should do that.

RHYS. You didn't like it?

ALISON. I didn't say I didn't like it. I just don't think it's a very good idea.

RHYS. Why not? Why isn't it a good idea?

ALISON. *(Looks at him, starts to say something, then seems to change her mind.)* I have to go.

(ALISON disappears into the darkness. RHYS stands there. Sound of owls.)

Scene 7

(GAVIN and BEL in the parlor.)

BEL. I've been talking with the new girl.

GAVIN. Have you?

BEL. I've been practicing not being crazy with her. She's quite an interesting person, actually. Rather easy to like. Not at all what I expected. Are you listening to me? I don't think you're listening to me.

GAVIN. I've done nothing but listen to you for the last twenty years.

BEL. Twenty-two. I'm a little disappointed that you've lost count. In any case, when Sarah goes, I think this girl might be a nice replacement for her.

GAVIN. You do?

BEL. She's a lovely creature, she seems not to mind working, and it will be a very good exercise for me, having her around to practice being sane with.

GAVIN. So now you don't think she's part of a curse?

BEL. I don't know what she is, but I like her.

GAVIN. Did you forget to take your medicine today?

BEL. Gavin, it might be a real breakthrough for me. For years I've been convinced that Morgan woman put a curse on us when she left, but now, when I look at this girl, who's so very much like her, and yet seems so innocent, I think perhaps I might have been mistaken. Whoever she is, she's just a girl. A very pretty girl, perhaps slightly insane, which is more or less what I was. I might enjoy taking her under my wing.

GAVIN. Your wing?

BEL. I've decided it's safe to presume she's not a succubus, or an incubus. I always get those two confused, but I don't think she's either one. Sarah has threatened to leave every day for the last two years, and nobody else wants to come out here. With our reputation, getting a girl with amnesia is a godsend.

GAVIN. You're sure that's what you want?

BEL. What's the matter? Don't you like her?

GAVIN. I like her fine. I just never in my wildest dreams imagined YOU would.

BEL. Well, I'm delighted to hear I'm not too old to surprise you now and then, big boy.

GAVIN. I'll talk to her about it.

BEL. Then it's settled.

GAVIN. I don't know that it's settled. I just said I'd talk to her.

BEL. You still seem to have reservations about her.

GAVIN. She is, after all, a complete stranger.

BEL. Well, who isn't? We are to her, as much as she is to us, and, for that matter, to each other. After all, we're married. How much stranger can you get? I was a stranger to you when you first met me, and I've grown stranger every year, but look how splendidly that turned out. Well, maybe that's not the best example. You don't want to throw that poor, homeless little waif out into the cold, do you?

GAVIN. No. I don't.

BEL. And you're not suggesting, I hope, that having a gorgeous young creature like that living under our roof would make me feel insecure, are you?

GAVIN. Of course not.

BEL. So you do think she's gorgeous?

GAVIN. She's young.

BEL. And I'm not?

GAVIN. You're beautiful. You always have been, and you always will be.

BEL. Horse puckey.

GAVIN. Bel, you've had your share of problems over the years, but physical unattractiveness has never been one of them.

BEL. So I'm only attractive to you physically?

GAVIN. I didn't say that.

BEL. I know you didn't love me when you married me, but I thought you'd learned to love me, over the years. I know I talk too much.

GAVIN. You don't talk too much.

BEL. Oh, shut up. I know it drives you crazy. I know you'd have killed me a long time ago except you're afraid I'd keep yapping at you from under the coffin lid.

GAVIN. Bel, I don't want to kill you. I love you.

BEL. But you do find that girl extremely attractive, don't you?

GAVIN. No.

BEL. Oh, come on, soldier. How could anybody not find her attractive? Maybe that's why you want to get rid of her.

GAVIN. I don't want to get rid of her.

BEL. Then swear. Swear to me that you don't want to get rid of her. Swear on the head of your son.

GAVIN. My son's not here. You want me to have him bring his head in here so I can swear on it?

BEL. Swear on my breast. Put your hand on my breast and swear you don't want to get rid of that girl.

GAVIN. *(Putting his hand on her breast.)* I swear I don't want to get rid of that girl.

BEL. Do you want to go upstairs and take a nap?

GAVIN. I'm not sleepy.

BEL. Neither am I.

GAVIN. All right.

BEL. You don't have to if you don't want to.

GAVIN. No, I want to.

BEL. You're just saying that.

GAVIN. I'm not just saying that.

BEL. Swear on my breast.

GAVIN. I just swore on your breast.

BEL. Swear on my other breast.

GAVIN. *(Putting his hand on her other breast.)* I swear I really want to go upstairs with you and not take a nap.

BEL. Well, that's very flattering, sweetie. Now, go find that girl and tell her the good news about her being welcome to stay here and live under my wing.

GAVIN. I thought we were going upstairs.

BEL. Is that all you can think about? You men are all alike. Animals. You go find that girl. I'm going in the kitchen and polish up the carving knives. You never know when you're going to have an uncontrollable urge to stick one into something, do you? Just kidding. Oh, and Gavin—

GAVIN. Yes?

BEL. You watch your step out there, killer.

(BEL gives him an extremely warm kiss, waves at him, then goes into the kitchen. GAVIN looks after her.)

GAVIN. Okay.

(The light fades on him.)

Scene 8

(Bird sounds. ALISON by the pond. GAVIN approaches her.)

GAVIN. You really like it out here, don't you?

ALISON. The pond seems to draw me towards it. I don't know why.

GAVIN. I've been going to have it drained for years.

ALISON. Why would you want to do that? It's so beautiful.

GAVIN. It's too deep out there. It's not safe.

ALISON. Nothing is safe.

GAVIN. Has my wife been bothering you?

ALISON. No. Not at all.

GAVIN. I don't want her bothering you.

ALISON. She's not bothering me. I like her.

GAVIN. She's not well.

ALISON. She's unhappy. Most people are. At least she's creative about it. It's all right. We get along.

GAVIN. Good. Has my son been bothering you?

ALISON. Of course not. Rhys is wonderful. He's a very good person.

GAVIN. Yes, but I don't want him bothering you.

ALISON. You don't seem to want anybody bothering me. In fact, you don't seem to want anybody getting anywhere near me. Just what do you want, Mr. Rose? Am I bothering you?

GAVIN. No. You're not bothering me.

ALISON. It's obvious that I am. It's been very nice of you to let me stay here at your house, but if you want me to leave now—

GAVIN. I don't want you to leave.

ALISON. But I do bother you, don't I?

GAVIN. You remind me of someone.

ALISON. Who do I remind you of?

GAVIN. It doesn't matter. It was a long time ago.

ALISON. Whoever it was, I'm not her. I'm somebody else entirely.

GAVIN. Sometimes I come upon you at a small distance, walking up the staircase or out here by the trees, and it's like seeing a ghost.

ALISON. I'm not a ghost. I'm flesh and blood. You can touch me if you want. See? *(She reaches out and touches his face with the palm of her hand.)* I'm warm. My hands are warm. Blood runs in me. If you prick me, I bleed. If you put your hand on my breast, you can feel my heart beating. I'm real. I hope that doesn't disappoint you. I hope you didn't want me to be a ghost.

GAVIN. *(Taking her hand from his face.)* No. I don't want you to be a ghost.

(He doesn't let go of her hand right away.)

>ALISON. You know who I am, don't you?
>GAVIN. Do I?
>ALISON. Yes. I think you do.
>GAVIN. Who are you?
>ALISON. Who do you want me to be?

(Pause. GAVIN lets go of her hand.)

>GAVIN. You can stay as long as you like. My wife wants you to stay. She just told me so. Sarah can use the help. I'll pay you, if you like. You're welcome here. But I would be careful, if I was you.
>ALISON. Careful of what? Of your wife?
>GAVIN. Among other things. She's rather unpredictable. And I'm never quite certain what's really going on in her mind.
>ALISON. But that's part of her charm, isn't it? Don't worry. I'll be careful.
>GAVIN. I hope so.

(They look at each other. GAVIN seems to be about to say something more, then thinks better of it, turns and goes. ALISON looks after him.)

Scene 9

(MATT at his desk. Music from the dance.)

>MATT. The night I returned from Maryland there was a dance in town, and I'd promised my wife we'd go. Sarah was there, with the lovesick Evan Unkefer, and Rhys brought Alison. There are certain

women, at a certain moment in their lives, that no man can keep from looking at, and that night Alison was such a woman. My wife saw me watching her. Alison smiled and waved from across the room. My wife looked at her. Alison looked back. She seemed to be about to come over to us, but then suddenly instead grabbed Rhys by the hand and pulled him out into the night.

(ALISON, pulling RHYS outside, night. She has actually pulled him from the darkness upstage to the point farthest down center.)

RHYS. You shouldn't come out here without your coat. You'll catch pneumonia.

ALISON. I'm hot from all the dancing. The air feels good. God, look at the stars. I must be red as a strawberry.

RHYS. You're incredibly beautiful.

ALISON. Oh, stop it.

RHYS. No man in that room has been able to take his eyes off you all night, and you know it.

ALISON. Even Matt Armitage?

RHYS. Especially Matt Armitage. And everyone knows how devoted he is to his wife.

ALISON. Is he? That's nice. I admire that. Although devotion is a recipe for misery. He seems to me to be a very sad man. Why is he so sad?

RHYS. He thinks too much.

ALISON. Maybe. His wife is lovely.

RHYS. Why don't you go over and meet her?

ALISON. I don't think she likes me.

RHYS. She doesn't know you. And why wouldn't she like you? Even my mother seems to like you. That in itself is an amazing achievement.

ALISON. I saw a bunch of girls in there looking daggers at me. Your old girlfriends, I presume.

RHYS. They were jealous because you're so beautiful. And

probably they were wondering who you are.

ALISON. Yes. Me too. Sarah's boyfriend adores her.

RHYS. I know. Poor Evan.

ALISON. I think he'd be very lucky to have her.

RHYS. She'll make his life a living hell.

ALISON. I know. He's committed an unforgivable sin—he loves her, but he's not the one she wants to love her. She'll make him pay dearly for that. But he's still lucky if he gets her.

RHYS. *(Pulling her towards him.)* Come here.

ALISON. *(Eluding him.)* No. I don't think you should kiss me while I'm still deciding who I am.

RHYS. You mean you get to choose who you are?

ALISON. I'm deciding that, too. I mean whether I can choose who I am, or if it's already out of my hands. Whether everything is chance and you can choose your own mask, or if God's already assigned you a mask you can't take off, in a play he wrote a long time ago. I'm not sure which is true yet, or which I want to be true.

RHYS. Maybe I can help you decide.

(He moves to kiss her again.)

ALISON. *(Pushing him away.)* I said no.

RHYS. I'm sorry.

ALISON. Oh, now I've hurt your feelings. I didn't mean to. It's just that—

(SARAH comes running out from the dance, crying and furious.)

SARAH. Stupid man. Stupid, stupid man.

RHYS. Sarah? What's the matter?

SARAH. Nothing's the matter. Leave me alone.

ALISON. Sarah, tell us what's wrong.

SARAH. Evan Unkefer's just done a horrible thing.

RHYS. What? What did he do?

SARAH. He asked me to marry him.

RHYS. What a cad. I'm going right in there and punch him in the nose.

SARAH. Don't make fun of me.

RHYS. That's all he did? Asked you to marry him? And you ran out bawling?

SARAH. No, first I punched him in the nose, then I ran out.

RHYS. Why did you punch him in the nose?

SARAH. Oh, he makes me so mad, mooning around after me like a moron.

ALISON. I'd think you might be just a little flattered.

SARAH. Yes, I should be flattered that while every other man in the room has his eyes glued on you all night, that cretin keeps following me around like a puppy, and then has the nerve to ask me to marry him.

RHYS. Did you say yes before you punched him?

SARAH. No, I said, Evan Unkefer, you're the stupidest man God ever made, and then I belted him one.

RHYS. So you think he'll take that as a definite no?

SARAH. I don't care how he takes it. *(She sees ALISON looking at her.)* What are you gawking at?

ALISON. I'm really sorry, Sarah.

SARAH. Sorry for what? That there's still one man left in town who's after somebody besides you? Don't worry. If he wasn't so nearsighted he'd be chasing you, too.

RHYS. Don't yell at Alison. She hasn't done anything.

SARAH. I'll yell at anybody I please. I do not work for your grotesque family tonight, Rhys. Tonight I am a perfectly free individual, and if I want to punch some jackass in the nose, that's my business.

ALISON. Rhys, I'm getting cold. I'm going inside. Why don't you stay out here with Sarah for a while?

SARAH. Oh, I wouldn't want to keep you two apart.

ALISON. It's all right. I want to go and meet Matt's wife. I'll see you two later.

(ALISON exchanges a look with RHYS behind SARAH's back, nodding in SARAH's direction, then goes back inside. SARAH and RHYS stand there, RHYS looking after ALISON.)

SARAH. Oh, go on in after her. I don't need you.

RHYS. I don't like it when you cry. It's not like you.

SARAH. I'm sorry I've failed to live up to your expectations.

RHYS. *(Coming over to put his arm around her.)* Whatever it is, it'll be all right.

SARAH. *(Pulling away from him.)* Get your filthy hands off me. This is no time to play doctor.

RHYS. I wasn't playing doctor, I was just—

SARAH. And how do you know it'll be all right? You don't know anything about it.

RHYS. Then tell me what's wrong with you.

SARAH. I'm just happy because I'm going to marry Evan Unkefer and have seventeen wall-eyed, stupid children.

RHYS. If you don't love him, don't marry him.

SARAH. Fine. And just who else do you think is ever going to want to marry me?

RHYS. Lots of people.

SARAH. Name one.

RHYS. Sarah, you're a very pretty girl, and a very smart one, and the best cook in the county. You can have anybody you want.

SARAH. Then I'll just take nobody, because that's what I'm going to get.

RHYS. You'll find somebody.

SARAH. No man is worth the aggravation. That's my conclusion.

RHYS. When I go to Yale, maybe I'll make a friend I can bring home for you.

SARAH. You try it and I'll shoot off the bastard's kneecap. You stupid son of a bitch.

RHYS. What? What did I do? I'm just trying to help.

SARAH. I don't need your help. Just get away from me. Get away.

(She is beating at him with her fists.)

RHYS. Hey. Stop that. Stop it. That hurts.

SARAH. *(Continuing to hit him.)* Good.

MATT. *(Coming out from the dance.)* What the hell's going on out here?

RHYS. She's beating the living daylights out of me, that's what's going on. God, talk about a bad mood.

SARAH. Get this idiot away from me, or I swear I'll kill him.

MATT. *(Restraining SARAH.)* Easy, kid. You've already broken one nose tonight. Rhys, why don't you go back in and try to save Alison from being trampled by people who want to dance with her? I'll keep Sarah company for a while.

SARAH. I don't need your babysitting, thank you.

MATT. You certainly need something.

RHYS. Okay. I'm going back in. But let me give you a safety tip, Matt. Whatever you do, don't propose to her. Somebody could get killed.

(RHYS goes back in.)

MATT. Rhys proposed to you?

SARAH. Evan Unkefer proposed to me. Stupid, stupid man.

MATT. You mean Evan, Rhys or me?

SARAH. I mean all of you. There isn't one of you with the brains of a fence post or the morals of a snake.

MATT. What did we do?

SARAH. Everything violent and rotten in the history of the universe.

MATT. With the possible exception of punching Evan Unkefer in the nose.

SARAH. Oh, he had it coming. And you're just as bad as the rest of them. Go away and leave me be.

MATT. I think you better tell me what's wrong.

SARAH. I'm getting married, that's what's wrong.

MATT. Well, uh, congratulations.

SARAH. Drop dead.

MATT. So this is just a case of premarital jitters? Is that it?

SARAH. Seventeen years old and I'm the only person in that house who can even counterfeit normal behavior. The mistress is a raving lunatic, the master broods and talks to himself, although I suppose I can understand that, since living with her could drive anybody over the edge. And Rhys is so infatuated with that terrible girl he found in the rain that he walks around the house all day with a silly grin on his face, bumping into things and treating me like I'm the cat. Well, I'm not the cat.

MATT. I never said you were the cat.

SARAH. And now they expect I'm just going to bounce right into Evan Unkefer's clammy bed and let her take my place. Well, I should. I should just pack up and leave them high and dry, and see how long they survive without me. There's so many damned rooms in that house, nobody can keep them all clean, nobody can even find them all, but does anybody ever lift a finger to help me? No. It's all up to Sarah. Sarah will take care of everything. A handful of people living in a house big enough for the Confederate Army and they expect that lazy girl to take care of it? They're so damned selfish. They take me for granted like they took my mother, worked her to death, and hardly noticed when she was gone. It'd serve them right if I married that stupid Unkefer boy and got out of that madhouse forever.

MATT. Sarah, whether you want to admit it or not, they'll survive without you.

SARAH. So you think I'm expendable, too, do you?

MATT. I think you deserve a life of your own. And since you've told them a hundred times you're leaving, they've grown to accept it. It doesn't mean they don't want you. If you don't want to go, just tell them.

SARAH. Of course I want to go. Why wouldn't I want to go? I envy you so much. You have a nice wife who loves you, and a house of your own, and the sweetest little boy. That Davey, he's a charmer. Stole my heart the first moment I saw him. Quiet little man, always reading books almost bigger than he is. I'd give anything for that.

MATT. Evan Unkefer is a pretty decent sort of fellow.

SARAH. He's a fool. Besides, he's got a broken nose.

MATT. You don't think you can love him?

SARAH. I don't see what difference it makes.

MATT. It would seem to me to make some difference.

SARAH. He'll do. I can handle him. He won't come home drunk and hit me like many I could name. I can have my way with him most of the time if I just pick at him and push him enough. What? What are you looking at?

MATT. Is that the kind of life you want?

SARAH. Since when has anybody around here ever taken a minute to think about what I want? It's better than most women I know will ever have. Why shouldn't I take it?

MATT. It's up to you, it's not up to me, but, Sarah, there are few things in this world more painful than being married to one person and loving someone else.

SARAH. And just how does that apply to my situation? And for that matter, what would you know about it?

MATT. You're right. I know nothing about anything.

SARAH. That must be why you're such a good lawyer.

(MATT smiles, puts his arm around her and kisses her forehead.)

MATT. Sarah, you're the best person I know.

SARAH. Yes, and a fat lot of good it does me. *(She wipes her eyes.)* Well, I'd better get back in there and survey the damage. People will think you and I've been out here smooching. Oh, what does it matter?

(She touches his arm, sighs a big sigh, and goes back upstage into the darkness. MATT stands there. The light fades on him.)

Scene 10

(BEL, in a white nightgown, in the midst of darkness, a small light before her, illuminating her face as if from a candle.)

BEL. Night in the dark old house. All in the dark the dragon's foul tongue speaks to me, whispers to go to her room. I slip out of bed, careful not to wake my foolish husband, and creep up the steps with my candle before me, all ahead and behind is darkness. The door to her room is not locked. I open it carefully and go in. Sound of the ticking clock by her bed. An owl in the tree by her window. At the foot of her bed I shine the candle down upon her. Oh, she is so lovely, sleeping there, I can hardly breathe. She looks so innocent. I want to hold her in my arms and comfort her, but the dragon whispers in my ear that she is the sorceress come back to kill us. Burn the witch, whispers the dragon. Burn the witch now. His breath is fire in my head. I hesitate, I resist. Innocent child. Dreaming of her lover, she cannot see his face. But I must be strong. Then another voice comes from the doorway, and it startles me, as anything that's not inside my head can startle me, and I turn briefly and there is Sarah, in her nightgown, Sarah, who hears everything in the house, whose job has always been to keep me out of trouble, my faithful protectress since she was a little girl, who heard me creeping up the steps or saw the light from the candle flash under her door as I passed by, and as I turn, the candle drops from my hand, not on the bed of the sleeping girl, but onto my own nightgown, and in a moment everything is fire, I am burning, breath of the dragon, burning from below, and somebody is screaming, it must be me, and then Sarah is screaming and then Alison is screaming and Sarah's trying to get me to roll on the floor, but the dragon whispers that the pond is cool and dark, so I smash through the ancient windowpane and roll down the steep roof, burning, and fall to the roof below it, burning, and then off again onto the grass, and then I am running and falling, stumbling and crawling towards the water, and the dragon's breath is roaring in my ears, and then there is the water and the ecstasy of darkness closing over me and the dragon has taken me into his mouth has entered into me has devoured me deep under the water, and the burning is gone, and there watching me in the water I see the eyes of the lost beloved dead I have come to join, and everything is lost, and somehow it is all quite perfect.

(The light fades on her and goes out.)

Scene 11

(RHYS in dim reddish lantern light in the Indian caves. ALISON appears, having come up the path to follow him.)

ALISON. Rhys?
RHYS. What are you doing here?
ALISON. What is this place?
RHYS. It's the Indian caves.
ALISON. I didn't know Indians lived in caves.
RHYS. These did. Delawares, I think. A long time ago. You can still find arrowheads and tools in here, and there's some paintings on

the wall farther back in there. Why did you follow me way out here?

ALISON. I was worried about you.

RHYS. This is where I come when I need to get away from things.

ALISON. Things like me?

RHYS. No. Not from you.

ALISON. Do you bring girls here?

RHYS. No.

ALISON. Has Sarah been here?

RHYS. Yes.

ALISON. Do you want me to go away so you can be alone?

RHYS. No.

ALISON. Then what do you want?

RHYS. Nothing.

ALISON. I wish I could help you. I want to help you. *(Pause.)* It wasn't my fault. What happened to your mother wasn't my fault.

RHYS. Nobody thinks it's your fault.

ALISON. I didn't do anything.

RHYS. I never said you did.

ALISON. I should leave this place and never come back. That would be the best thing.

RHYS. I don't want you to leave.

ALISON. You never should have brought me in out of the rain.

RHYS. I have a hopeless weakness for strays, like my mother did. She was a lost creature herself. My father rescued her from the war, and, for a while, to some extent, from her madness, but in the end nobody can rescue anybody. There are too many consequences, and the consequences accumulate and drown you. I'll bet you a hundred years from now the descendants of Mother's rescued animals will still be multiplying in abandoned parts of the house. There are pigeons and whippoorwills living in the attic. It's always been a haunted place. Some day I'll haunt it.

ALISON. I don't belong in that house.

RHYS. Alison, if you want to help me, promise me something.

ALISON. What? Anything you want.

RHYS. Promise me you'll never leave us. Promise me you'll stay here always. Will you promise me that?

ALISON. Are you sure that's what you want?

RHYS. Yes. I'm sure.

ALISON. Then I will. I'll stay. I'll always stay. I promise. *(He looks at her. She looks away.)* We should be getting back now.

RHYS. Not yet.

ALISON. It's getting very dark out. I'm not sure I can find my way back alone. I just followed you. I wasn't watching where I was going. I never do. The truth is, I'm lost. I'm completely lost.

RHYS. No you're not.

(He kisses her. She pulls away.)

ALISON. Rhys, that really isn't a good idea. You don't know— *(He kisses her again. She pulls away again. They look at each other.)* You don't know what you're doing. You have no idea what you're doing here. This is not what you think. This is—

(Pause. Then she kisses him. The light fades on them and goes out.)

End of Act I

TRISTAN

ACT II

Scene 12

(Sound of a ticking clock in the darkness. Lights up slowly on MATT at his desk, RHYS on the porch, ALISON sitting on the bed, SARAH in the kitchen, GAVIN by the pond, and BEL, dressed in white, sitting on the center of the sofa in the parlor, looking radiant and quite serene.)

BEL. There are numerous advantages to being dead. For one thing, you can see everybody and everything any time you want, and nobody bothers you except the living, who are rather tiresome but nevertheless do retain a kind of bizarre fascination for some of us. On the whole, though, I often wonder how the living manage to stand each other.

ALISON. The house is so vast.

BEL. The living appear to the dead as a confused jumble of voices, past, present and future, like an after dinner sleep, dreaming of these and of things that never were and never will be.

MATT. As I attempt to make sense of the fragments of time and memory all crowding in—

BEL. They are lost in a labyrinth of voices.

RHYS. So many accumulated rooms over the years, rooms once lived in, or never lived in, rooms abandoned, rooms reclaimed for a time and then lost again.

ALISON. He gave me wine, that first night, a glass of wine to warm me.

RHYS. I can still see her in the rain.

ALISON. I wouldn't drink at first, so he drank from the glass, and then so did I, and from that moment we were lost.

SARAH. Stupid men. Stupid, stupid men.

GAVIN. Of the matter of the burning of flesh I once kissed—

ALISON. I dreamed there was something in the woods. In the dark, in the snow.

GAVIN. I remember a small, mad girl, lost by the ruins of a tent in the woods long ago.

ALISON. It was breathing, and it crashed through the downstairs window and came up the steps, like a pig, only hairy, with long backwards tusks, and it jumped on the bed and attacked me, it was goring me, blood was everywhere, there was a ring of flour around the bed, and the flour was spattered with blood.

GAVIN. Lost creature, rescued from darkness, then brought to this dark place.

MATT. A wilderness of voices.

GAVIN. She falls in fire from the battlements.

BEL. All crowding in like the voices of the dead, for the dead still have nightmares, but do not pity them, for if just once you are foolish enough to allow yourself to pity them, then you become one of them, and you are lost in the labyrinth of voices forever.

(The light fades on them and goes out.)

TRISTAN 51

Scene 13

(SARAH working in the kitchen. ALISON is coming down the stairs and through the parlor, past BEL, who throughout this act will wander about the house, watching the scenes as they play.)

SARAH. Oh, so the Empress of the Moon finally sees fit to grace us with her presence. Don't mind me, your majesty. You just have a seat and watch me work. I'm used to it.

ALISON. I'm sorry, Sarah. I haven't been feeling well.

SARAH. Yes, me neither. Work isn't half so much fun once you've actually got to do some, is it?

ALISON. I'm not being lazy. I'm ill.

SARAH. You look healthy enough to me. You say you're going to help me around here and then you take to laying in bed half the day like Mrs. Casey's pregnant sow.

ALISON. I get dizzy when I stand up, and I've been sick to my stomach in the mornings.

SARAH. For a girl who's not been feeling well, you've certainly been eating like a horse. You've been bolting down enough food for two people. *(Pause. SARAH looks at her.)* You're sick in the mornings?

BEL. Uh oh.

ALISON. Usually in the mornings, yes.

SARAH. Has your friend paid you a visit this month?

ALISON. What friend?

SARAH. You know what I'm talking about. Did it come this month, or didn't it?

ALISON. I really don't think that's any of your business.

SARAH. Just how late are you, Alison?

ALISON. Kind of late. Very late. Actually, I've missed two of them.

SARAH. My God. He's put a child in you.

ALISON. Who? No.

SARAH. You're telling me it's impossible?

ALISON. Yes. Well, no. But—

SARAH. You filthy little trollop. You waltz in here, take my place, kill the mistress, and now you're carrying her son's bastard child.

ALISON. I didn't kill anybody. You saw what happened.

SARAH. Unless of course it doesn't belong to Rhys. I suppose it might just as well have been a traveling pots and pans salesman, or the preacher, or Matt Armitage, for that matter. Every man within smelling range has been hot as a dog after you since the night of your grand arrival.

ALISON. Sarah, that's not fair.

SARAH. Oh, it's not fair, is it? Well, why don't you just tell me what's fair, then? You've got exactly what you wanted, you dirty, scheming little slut.

ALISON. I don't know what you're talking about. And stop calling me names.

SARAH. You wanted him and you got him, and now you're carrying what you'd like us to believe is his child, so now you can take over the whole damned place, is that right?

ALISON. I don't want to take over anything.

SARAH. Oh, come on. Do you think I'm as stupid as they are?

GAVIN. *(Entering.)* Is all this yelling really necessary? What are you two caterwauling about now?

ALISON. Nothing.

SARAH. Nothing except that your son has apparently got this pathetic little strumpet with child.

ALISON. Sarah—

GAVIN. Is that true? Alison?

ALISON. It seems likely that I might be expecting, yes.

GAVIN. And you're sure it belongs to Rhys?

TRISTAN 53

ALISON. What kind of question is that?
GAVIN. Is it my son's child or isn't it?
ALISON. Yes. It is.
GAVIN. Jesus Christ.
ALISON. I'm sorry.
GAVIN. How on earth could you let a thing like that happen?
ALISON. I don't know. He was grieving. I wanted to comfort him.
SARAH. Yes, you're a regular sister of mercy, aren't you?
GAVIN. This is my fault. I let you stay here. I knew it was a mistake, but I let you stay anyway. I've done this. It's my doing.
SARAH. It's not your doing, it's hers. Can't you see she's planned it this way?
GAVIN. Sarah, please.
SARAH. Well, why do all you men keep trying to make excuses for her? She's killed your wife and seduced your son, and all you can do is jump in to take the blame for it yourself.
GAVIN. Sarah, will you just shut up a minute? You don't understand this.
SARAH. I understand it a good deal better than you do. And I won't stay here and be talked to that way any longer. I quit.
GAVIN. You're not going anywhere. Now sit down and be quiet for a minute. I need you.
SARAH. You need me for what? To keep on being your household slave until I drop dead some day face down in my oatmeal?
GAVIN. To be the only person in this house I can count on. Will you just sit down a minute please and let me think?
SARAH. Fine. Don't strain yourself.

(She sits.)

GAVIN. Does Rhys know?
ALISON. No. Not yet.

GAVIN. Good. You're not going to tell him.

ALISON. If I'm going to be having his child, I've got to tell him sooner or later.

GAVIN. You can't tell him, and you know why you can't.

SARAH. I don't know why she can't.

GAVIN. Sarah—

SARAH. All right, all right.

ALISON. If I don't tell him, then what am I supposed to do?

GAVIN. Have you been to a doctor about this?

ALISON. No.

GAVIN. Come on, then. We're going into town to see Doc McGort.

ALISON. And then what?

GAVIN. Just come along and you'll find out. Sarah, you stay here, and if Rhys asks where we are, tell him we went to do some shopping. And don't you say one word to him about this other matter, have you got that?

SARAH. She's right. You can't keep it a secret for long. Isn't it better if—

GAVIN. Will you let me handle it? Just don't tell Rhys, and make sure he doesn't go into town until I've come back, is that clear?

SARAH. I don't like keeping things from Rhys.

GAVIN. Just do it for now, and when I get back we can talk about it. Can I count on you or not?

SARAH. I suppose so.

GAVIN. Thank you. *(He turns to ALISON.)* All right. You. Come on.

ALISON. I don't know if I—

GAVIN. *(Grabbing her by the arm and pulling her from the sofa.)* Just come on. Get a move on.

ALISON. Hey. I don't feel good.

GAVIN. You're going to feel a hell of a lot worse if you don't go out there and get in that buggy right now.

ALISON. All right. I'm going. I've never seen you act like this. Sarah, listen—
GAVIN. We've no time to waste jabbering with Sarah. Sarah is fine. Now, come on.

(GAVIN pushes ALISON out the door. SARAH is left alone in the parlor, except for the ghost of BEL, who watches her sadly.)

SARAH. Yes. Sarah is fine. Sarah is always fine. Sarah takes care of everybody and everything. She's only a girl, but in her soul she's the old woman she knows she'll be soon enough. We can always count on Sarah.
MATT. *(At his desk, drinking.)* More and more, these long nights, I think of Sarah, a lovely young woman, very smart and strong, and of all the days and nights she would spend in that big, dark house, cleaning up after these lost people, trapped in a labyrinth of nightmares not of her making. Who was ever there for her? Not me.

(He drinks.)

BEL. *(Stroking SARAH's hair tenderly.)* Poor child. I took you for granted when I was alive. Isn't that always the way? Labyrinth of desire. Lost.

(BEL puts her arm around SARAH and kisses her hair, as if comforting a child. SARAH does not appear to notice.)

Scene 14

(Some hours later. Sarah is sewing on the sofa in the parlor. RHYS enters.)

RHYS. Where is everybody?
SARAH. They've gone to town.
RHYS. What for?
SARAH. Shopping. They've gone shopping.
RHYS. My father and Alison went shopping together?
SARAH. Yes.
RHYS. How long have they been gone?
SARAH. I don't know. Two or three hours.
RHYS. That's odd.
SARAH. Why is that odd?
RHYS. They never go to town together. Alison always goes with me or you.
SARAH. Well, sometimes, Rhys, things don't happen the way you expect them to.
RHYS. I guess not. What's the matter?
SARAH. Nothing's the matter. Why should anything be the matter? Why do you always ask me what's the matter?
RHYS. Come on, Sarah. I know you. What's wrong? Has Evan Unkefer jilted you for crazy Annie the pig girl?
SARAH. Why don't you just go away and leave me alone? *(She pricks her finger.)* OWWWW. Now see what you made me do? Son of a bitch.
RHYS. Watch your language. What kind of girl talks like that? Are you crying?
SARAH. I've stuck my finger with the needle. Do you mind if I cry while I bleed?
RHYS. Let me see it.

TRISTAN

SARAH. Don't touch me.
RHYS. What did I do now?
SARAH. When are you going to learn that my world does not revolve entirely around you? Believe it or not, there are things going on in people's lives that have absolutely nothing whatever to do with you. Or is your walnut sized brain too small to handle that concept?
RHYS. I'm just trying to help. What do you want from me?
SARAH. I want you to get away from me and stay away. I want to be as far away from you as possible. I'm sick to death of you, all right?
RHYS. Sarah, whatever it is, when you're ready to tell me about it, I'll be here, because no matter what you say or how much you fuss at me you're the best friend I have in the world. You always have been, and you always will be.
SARAH. Well, what a tremendous honor that is. I'm thrilled. I'm completely overwhelmed. Catch me while I faint. Get me a bucket before I lose my breakfast.

(RHYS looks at her. GAVIN enters.)

RHYS. There you are. Where have you been?
GAVIN. In town.
RHYS. With Alison?
GAVIN. Yes, with Alison.
RHYS. Well, where is she?
GAVIN. I need to talk to you.
RHYS. Is she hiding? She didn't fall off the wagon on the way home, did she?
GAVIN. Just forget about Alison for a minute.
SARAH. You did bring her back, didn't you?
RHYS. Why wouldn't he bring her back?
SARAH. What did you do with her?
GAVIN. Sarah, why don't you leave us alone for a minute?

SARAH. Whatever that girl's done, you can't just throw her out in the cold again with nobody to—

GAVIN. Sarah, will you let me talk to my son?

RHYS. Will somebody tell me where Alison is?

ALISON. *(Entering.)* I'm right here. Where should I be?

GAVIN. Rhys, Alison and I have something to tell you.

RHYS. That sounds awfully serious. What is this? Some sort of conspiracy? Everybody's acting very strange today. Sarah's furious, you two run off to town and she's afraid you haven't brought Alison back. What's going on here?

GAVIN. Alison and I have gotten married.

RHYS. I beg your pardon?

GAVIN. Married. Alison and I. Have gotten married.

RHYS. To each other?

GAVIN. To each other. We're man and wife now.

RHYS. She can't be your wife. That's crazy. You can't just go into town one day and get married. Don't you have to get a license and then wait or something?

GAVIN. My grandfather owned this town. I can do anything I want.

RHYS. Alison, you didn't really just go into town and marry my father, did you?

ALISON. Yes. I did.

RHYS. Why in God's name would you want to do a thing like that?

ALISON. He asked me.

RHYS. He asked you, so you married him? What the hell kind of sense does that make?

ALISON. Don't yell at me. I don't feel good.

RHYS. What have you two been doing? Carrying on together all this time behind my back?

ALISON. No.

RHYS. That's it. It's got to be it. All the time you've been with me, you've also been sleeping with my father.

ALISON. I have not been sleeping with your father.

GAVIN. Rhys, just calm down.

RHYS. Hell, you've probably been sleeping with Matt Armitage, too. Maybe your real goal is to bed down every man in Pendragon County.

ALISON. I have never in my life been with anybody but you.

RHYS. Then why did you just run off and marry my father?

ALISON. You're going to college soon. The odds are very good that you'll forget all about me when you get there. I didn't know what would happen to me when you left. This seemed like a very sensible solution.

RHYS. Yes, I guess it was. Everything here is in Dad's name, isn't it?

GAVIN. Rhys—

RHYS. No, that's all right. It's fine with me. Maybe I'd better leave you two alone so you can get upstairs and start your honeymoon. Unless you'd like Sarah and me to go in the kitchen so you can do it right here on the sofa.

GAVIN. That's enough.

RHYS. Oh, sorry. Got to watch my manners. What was I thinking? The two most important people in my life have just betrayed me, and here I am, forgetting my manners.

GAVIN. I know you don't think so now, but you'll just have to trust me that this is the best thing for everybody concerned.

RHYS. Well, for you, maybe. God, my mother isn't even cold in her grave. How could you do that?

GAVIN. I don't have to justify my actions to you.

RHYS. Fine. It doesn't matter. It's time I got the hell out of this place, anyway.

GAVIN. You're not going anywhere.

RHYS. Just who is going to stop me? You?

ALISON. Rhys, don't do anything stupid.

RHYS. Right. You've just run off and tied the knot with old Dad. God forbid I should do anything stupid.

ALISON. I don't want you to be hurt. I just—

RHYS. *(Pushing her away.)* Get away from me.

GAVIN. Let her alone.

RHYS. You don't tell me what to do any more.

ALISON. Stop it.

RHYS. What's the matter, Mrs. Rose? You getting anxious to get upstairs with old Dad? I hope he can still keep you satisfied.

GAVIN. You will not speak to her that way, is that clear?

RHYS. That's great, Dad. Defend her honor. Except what the hell kind of honor can she have?

ALISON. I'm going upstairs.

RHYS. *(Grabbing ALISON by the shoulders.)* What do you think, you can just play with people like that? You think there aren't any consequences?

GAVIN. *(Pulling RHYS away from ALISON.)* Get your hands off her.

RHYS. Let go of me.

SARAH. Rhys—

RHYS. Just get away from me.

(RHYS pushes GAVIN away. GAVIN stumbles back, off balance, and hits his head on the cabinet upstage.)

SARAH. Just stop. Now, stop.

ALISON. Rhys, you've hurt him.

RHYS. Nothing hurts him. Nothing touches him. Nothing ever has.

ALISON. He's not moving.

SARAH. *(Kneeling down to look at GAVIN.)* Mr. Rose? Are you all right?

GAVIN. I'm fine.

TRISTAN

SARAH. You've got a terrible gash in your forehead.
GAVIN. I hit it on the cabinet. I'm all right.

(He starts to get up.)

SARAH. Don't get up yet. Wait a minute.
GAVIN. Sarah, I'm all right, dammit.

(GAVIN staggers to his feet, holding his forehead, which is bloody.)

SARAH. You're going to fall again.
GAVIN. I'm not going to fall.
ALISON. You're bleeding. Be still a minute. *(To RHYS:)* Do you see what you've done? Do you see?
GAVIN. All right, Rhys. If you want to leave, I won't try and stop you. Just get out of my house.
SARAH. Don't say things you don't mean, and sit down before you fall down.
GAVIN. God dammit, Sarah, will you stop fussing at me? I'm going upstairs.

(GAVIN staggers and falls on the steps, SARAH and ALISON helping to catch him.)

SARAH. Stubborn. Stupid and stubborn.
ALISON. Sarah, go into town and fetch the doctor.
GAVIN. I don't need any damned doctor.
ALISON. Sarah, go on. I'll take care of him.
SARAH. I'm not leaving him with you.
RHYS. You stay here, Sarah. I'll go.
GAVIN. Yes, go. And don't bother to come back.

(GAVIN staggers up the steps to the bedroom with the help of the two

women. ALISON looks back at RHYS. SARAH does not. RHYS looks up the steps, then turns and goes.)

Scene 15

(As ALISON and SARAH help GAVIN to lie down on the bed, BEL speaks.)

BEL. Having had such a wonderful opportunity to observe the living so closely after my untimely but spectacular demise, I'm finding myself more and more both fascinated and appalled by their almost complete inability to focus on what actually matters in any given situation. Once you're dead, this is no longer a problem. You can focus remarkably well from inside a coffin—I mean on the basic themes and images, the central line of action in the complex and multileveled theatre, upon what's left when the body decomposes and all else, quite literally, falls away. Now, look at this, for example. The woman comes between, the son nearly kills the father. I know this story. I'm sure it must have been in one of my crazy father's books, before we fed it to the goat, or maybe we saw it that time we went up to Cleveland to hear that woman with the huge ass shrieking opera. We live out these patterns. Our lives are an infinitely complex series of interlocking plays, stretching back and forth through time to infinity, the major characters of one play being the spear-carriers in another. We're the stories the old women tell by the fire on winter evenings. We play in comedy one night, tragedy the next, sometimes both at the same time. I've allowed one of these men to ejaculate into my body, and been kicked in the stomach from the inside by the other one, and then pushed him out into the world amid the damnedest screaming bloody mess you ever saw, but I pity most the women, who carry the massive burden of life inside them, all to be lost, all lost. It's rather beautiful, when viewed from a certain aesthetic distance, but when you get up close you can't see anything. Life is too close while we're living it to make any sense out of. Death gives us a much better perspective, but by then it's too late to do a damned thing about anything. And that's the beauty of it. All lost things are beautiful, and all beautiful things are lost. What a shame. And yet, how interesting.

Scene 16

(RHYS on the porch. MATT comes out of the house.)

RHYS. Is he all right?

MATT. Doc says he seems to be. He took a really nasty blow to the head. You might have killed him, you know.

RHYS. I wasn't trying to kill him.

MATT. Then maybe you should go up there and tell him that.

RHYS. I'm leaving.

MATT. You can't leave now. You're needed here.

RHYS. He doesn't need me. He's got her. There's nothing here for me any more. Did you know they were getting married?

MATT. Not until this afternoon.

RHYS. I don't understand it. Do you understand it?

MATT. All explanations are lies.

RHYS. It's better if I leave. They don't want me here.

MATT. Everybody wants you here.

RHYS. I'd be going away to college soon, anyway.

MATT. Then wait, and go when you planned on going. Don't leave things like this. You'll regret it.

RHYS. How do you know what I'll regret? The old lecher's got what he wants, and so does she.

MATT. You're being harder on them than they deserve.

RHYS. I don't know why you're trying to defend them. Hasn't she been seducing you all the time she's been after my father and me?

MATT. That's a lie.

RHYS. It's not a lie. I've seen you with her. How did you manage to get so damned chummy with her so soon? I saw your face, the day you looked through the law office window at her.

MATT. Rhys, you're making a mistake here, and I don't want you going away from this place thinking you know what you don't know.

RHYS. I know you wanted her, too, from the first minute you saw her there at the window.

MATT. That wasn't the first time I saw her.

RHYS. What do you mean?

MATT. I mean I've known her all her life.

RHYS. How could you know her all her life?

MATT. Your father's been supporting Alison and her mother and sister for years.

RHYS. What are you talking about?

MATT. There's a house in Maryland. Your great-grandfather Zach used to stop there on his way to Washington. He left it to his son John, who left it to your father. Your family's been supporting them there for a long time.

RHYS. Why would Zach and John and my father want to support a bunch of women in Maryland? What is it? A whore house?

MATT. No, it's not a whore house.

RHYS. Then what is it?

MATT. Listen to me, and try to follow this. Your father's mother was a servant in this house. After he was born, Zach Pendragon paid a man named Robey to take her to Maryland and look after his house there. When Robey died, your grandmother came back to Armitage, and she and your grandfather John got together again, briefly, and Alison was the result.

RHYS. I don't follow that.

MATT. Alison is the daughter of your grandparents. She's your father's sister.

RHYS. That doesn't make any sense. How the hell do you know what she is?

MATT. When his father died, Gavin didn't want to have anything more to do with any of this, so he asked my father to take care of them and never mention it to him again. Gavin supplied the money. My father sent it to a bank in Maryland. Your grandmother and her daughters took care of the house there, and at least two or three times a year my father would stop there on his way to or from Washington or New York, to make sure everything was all right, and he'd usually take me with him.

RHYS. You knew all this time and you never told me?

MATT. When my father died, and I took over the law practice, I inherited that job, too. Gavin didn't want you involved with any of that. When Alison's mother died, and she showed up here, I didn't know what to do. I felt sorry for her. She wanted a little time to get to know her family.

RHYS. Well, she's certainly accomplished that, hasn't she? And my father knew who she was all along?

MATT. I think he did. He never asked me.

RHYS. But if he knew she's his sister, why would he marry her?

MATT. To keep her away from you.

RHYS. And she knows, and she still—

MATT. Yes.

RHYS. How could she do this?

MATT. You'd have to ask her that. She's always been—

(ALISON appears from the house. MATT stops in mid-sentence. They look at each other for a moment.)

ALISON. He's sleeping now. Sarah's with him. *(Pause.)* Matt, I need to talk to Rhys.

MATT. I've told him.

ALISON. Told him what?

MATT. About who you are.

ALISON. Why did you do that?

MATT. I thought he should know.

ALISON. What else did you tell him?

RHYS. You mean there's more?

MATT. I told him who you are. The rest is up to you.

ALISON. Fine. Now leave us alone so I can talk to him. It's all right. He's not going to hurt me.

MATT. I'll be right inside.

(He goes into the house.)

RHYS. So I guess, as near as I can figure it, that makes you my aunt, is that right?

ALISON. I don't know what it makes me.

RHYS. It also makes you a liar and a whore who's managed to con me into committing incest and then married my father, who just happens to be her brother.

ALISON. Rhys—

RHYS. Just what did you think you were doing? Did you come here on purpose to destroy us? Wasn't it enough what you did to my mother? Did you have to marry my father, too?

ALISON. Just listen. Will you please just listen to me?

RHYS. Fine. I'd certainly be fascinated to hear what you could possibly come up with that would explain what you've done to anybody's satisfaction.

ALISON. My mother raised me to hate you people. She said this house was mine, as much as any of yours, and she raised me to come back here and claim my share of it. And when she died, I guess that's what I came here to do. It's hard for me to be sure.

RHYS. You had it all planned.

ALISON. I didn't plan anything. I just got on the train and came here. I didn't know what I was going to do when I got here. I just needed to see the place my mother had told me about since I was a little girl. It was like this dark, terrible fairy tale she'd tell me at night, about this wonderful old house and the terrible people who lived in it. I came here because I promised her I would. But I never planned anything. And I certainly didn't plan on feeling this way about you.

RHYS. What are you trying to say, Alison? You love me, so you married my father? Is that about it?

ALISON. Your father and I made an agreement. He would marry me and make sure I was taken care of for the rest of my life. I would have a home here. And he would never touch me.

RHYS. So you'd get my inheritance, and what would he get?

ALISON. I'd get MY inheritance, not yours. Just what's coming to me. And he'd get—he'd make it impossible for you and I to ever get together again except as family. As friends. The way it really has to be from now on.

RHYS. He married you to save me?

ALISON. To save us both. From something we felt for each other that we never should have felt, and that we mustn't let ourselves feel any more.

RHYS. You expect me to believe that?

ALISON. You can believe it or not believe it. It's true.

RHYS. If you want the place so damned much, you can have it. I'm getting out of here.

ALISON. Where are you going?

RHYS. I don't see what difference it makes. Jesus, why the hell would I want to stay here now?

ALISON. Because your father needs you. And I need you.

RHYS. I don't see what for. You've got what you wanted.

ALISON. I don't know what I wanted. I just don't want to lose you.

RHYS. What did you think I'd do when I found out you'd married my father? Did you think I'd smile and wish you good luck? Did you expect me to throw rice at the wedding? I don't remember getting an invitation. Maybe you thought you could just go right on sleeping with your stepson after the wedding. Or your nephew, whichever you prefer.

ALISON. I didn't want to hurt you. I'm sorry. I don't feel good.

RHYS. I don't feel so great myself. I've got to pack.

ALISON. At least stop and see your father before you go.

RHYS. Matt said he's all right.

ALISON. You can't just leave without talking to him. You've got to at least try and make it right.

RHYS. It will never be right. Do you understand that? No matter how long we live, it will never be right.

(SARAH comes out onto the porch. RHYS looks at her, then goes past her and into the house.)

SARAH. Did you tell him?

ALISON. About what?

SARAH. About the baby, of course.

ALISON. No. And you're not going to tell him, either.

SARAH. It's his baby. He has a right to know.

ALISON. Sarah, we are not going to tell him. He's leaving.

SARAH. He can't leave. Where is he going?

ALISON. I don't know, but we're not telling him about the baby.

SARAH. If you don't tell him, I will.

ALISON. Sarah, if you love him, get him to go up and see his father. He's got to talk to Gavin before he leaves. Can you get him to do that?

SARAH. You sound like you want him to leave.

ALISON. I don't want him to leave, but if he does leave, I want him to leave with things all right between him and his father.

SARAH. But if we tell him about the baby, maybe he'll stay.

ALISON. Do you want him to stay here knowing he's fathered a child on his father's wife? Do you want that hell for him?

(SARAH looks at her. RHYS reappears with a traveling bag.)

SARAH. Well, that was quick. Traveling light, are we?

RHYS. There's nothing here I want. Sarah, you'll have to take care of things now. I know you will. You always do.

SARAH. Do you think you can just run off and leave everything in my lap like this? Leave me your mess to clean up?

RHYS. If you don't want to be here, then marry Evan Unkefer and get out, or marry somebody else, or get a job somewhere else, I don't know.

SARAH. And you don't care, either.

RHYS. I didn't say that. I didn't mean that.

SARAH. If you're going, at least go up and see your father first.

RHYS. I don't want to see my father.

SARAH. Whatever has happened, he's your father, and he loves you, and you've just nearly killed him. Do you want that to be the last memory he has of his son?

(RHYS hesitates. Then he puts down the bag and goes in slowly and up the steps to see his father.)

Scene 17

(GAVIN lying on the bed. RHYS approaches, stands there. Pause.)

GAVIN. I remember when I was stronger than you. It wasn't all that long ago.
RHYS. I didn't mean to hurt you.
GAVIN. No.
RHYS. I just wanted to make sure you're all right before I go.
GAVIN. Where are you going?
RHYS. New York, I suppose.
GAVIN. What's in New York?
RHYS. A number of things.
GAVIN. Name one.
RHYS. Newspapers.
GAVIN. What about them?
RHYS. I thought I might work for one.
GAVIN. Why?
RHYS. I don't know. This house has been my entire universe for much too long. I want to go places and investigate some things.
GAVIN. What things?
RHYS. I don't know yet.
GAVIN. What about Yale?
RHYS. I think I need to be in the real world.
GAVIN. Yale is real.
RHYS. Not very.
GAVIN. You seem to think you know a lot about places you've never been to.
RHYS. You've never been there, either.
GAVIN. This is true. Your grandfather went to Yale, and your great-grandfather Zach. But I was the bastard child. Everybody knew, but nobody said. That was our way. At least he put me in the will. "To

my son, Gavin," it said. I can still hear old Jake Armitage reading those words out. My father could write it in his will for his lawyer to say, but he could never say it himself. So I inherited this house, and several battalions of ghosts, family secrets and nightmares. I have it, but I've never felt like I belonged here. I didn't want you to feel that way. I was hoping you'd grow up with the illusion that you belonged to a place. But the inertia of events has a way of subverting all one's plans. That too is part of your checkered heritage. There are many things you don't know.

RHYS. Matt told me about Alison.

GAVIN. Matt told you what about Alison?

RHYS. Who she is, and where she came from. Were you never going to tell me?

GAVIN. What would have been the point of that?

RHYS. Did you like being left in the dark by your own father?

GAVIN. No. Well, yes, in a way. There are some distinct advantages to living in the dark. We are all left in the dark to some extent. Most of the universe is darkness. I don't know that I'd have been happier the other way. I'm not sure there is another way. All light is temporary.

RHYS. I have to go now.

GAVIN. You don't have to go.

RHYS. I can't stay here after this.

GAVIN. This is your home.

RHYS. Not right now it isn't.

GAVIN. It always was. It always will be. You might think you can leave it, but you're very much mistaken.

RHYS. Maybe at some point I can come back.

GAVIN. You will never leave.

RHYS. Goodbye.

GAVIN. You will never leave this place. *(RHYS goes down the steps.)* You will never leave.

Scene 18

(ALISON, SARAH and MATT are waiting in the parlor. RHYS comes down the steps.)

RHYS. All right. We've talked. Now I'm going.

(He picks up his bag, looks at them, hesitates.)

SARAH. Well, fine, then. If you're going, go. You won't get the satisfaction of seeing any tears from me.

(RHYS puts down his bag and walks over in their direction. ALISON tenses, but he goes past her to SARAH.)

RHYS. Sarah—
SARAH. *(Eluding his grasp.)* No touching. I do not require any touching, thank you. If you want to go off and leave us, fine, you do what you please, but I don't need any hugs from you to make you feel better about it. I don't want to pretend it's all right. If you want to hug somebody, go and hug your stepmother over there. She's the big expert on physical contact.
RHYS. *(Looking at ALISON, then back to SARAH.)* I'll write.
SARAH. I hope you don't expect me to answer you.
ALISON. I'll answer you.
RHYS. I'll write to Sarah.
SARAH. I'll throw them in the garbage.
ALISON. No she won't.
SARAH. Write to your father.
RHYS. Just to you, Sarah.

(He picks up his bag.)

TRISTAN

MATT. Do you need some money?
RHYS. I don't need anything from you.

(He looks at them for a moment, then turns and goes out the door and disappears into the darkness. Pause.)

SARAH. Well. I've got supper to make. I don't suppose anybody's going to help me.
ALISON. I'll help you in a minute, Sarah.
SARAH. Yes, I've heard that one before, haven't I?

(She goes into the kitchen. ALISON stands there a moment, looking at MATT.)

MATT. Maybe it's for the best.
ALISON. Stay for supper if you like. I'm going up to sit with my husband.

(MATT looks at her. She goes up the steps to GAVIN. MATT watches her, then turns and moves downstage.)

Scene 19

(MATT drinking at his desk.)

MATT. When Rhys was gone, a part of me was pleased. I was ashamed of that feeling, but it was there, and my wife knew. She always knew, but she never said. I would go out to that old Gothic nightmare house, bats flying out from it at dusk, crows in the woods on either side of the long, rutted lane that led to her, and even though she was married to my friend and carried within her the child of his son, and despite the love I felt for my wife and the relentless eyes of my child, each time I made that journey through dark woods I felt, combined with dread and shame, an intense sexual excitement, because to go out to that house was to see her again. And I was needed. Rhys was gone and they needed me more than ever now, for although it looked at first as if no serious harm was done when Gavin hit his head, after Rhys left for New York, Gavin began to act rather strangely.

(ALISON is coming down the steps. SARAH comes out of the kitchen.)

SARAH. Where has he got to now?

ALISON. I don't know. I thought he was with you.

SARAH. You were supposed to watch him.

ALISON. I can't keep track of him all the time. Sarah, he's a grown man. Why do we have to watch him constantly?

SARAH. Because he's not right in the head.

ALISON. He seems all right to me.

SARAH. A great lot of attention you pay to him. The second Mrs. Rose, such a loving little wife. You eat all day, look out the window and talk to your stomach.

ALISON. I think it's good to talk to your unborn child. It gets him used to the world before he enters it.

SARAH. I wouldn't tell yours too much about this place, or it might not want to come out. Where IS that man?

ALISON. Don't worry about Gavin. He'll be fine.

SARAH. He's behaving like a lunatic. He talks to himself all the time now.

ALISON. Well, you talk to yourself.

SARAH. Yes, but at least I'm listening.

ALISON. He's lost his wife and his son. Give him some time.

SARAH. He's your husband now, as appalling a situation as that may be. Don't you care what happens to him?

ALISON. I can't tell him where to go or what to do or not to talk to himself. If you want to follow him around all day, that's up to you. I can't.

SARAH. Yes, you've got much more important things to do, like eat an entire roast chicken and moon about Rhys. Just because you've got a baby in you doesn't mean you get to sit around here all day like a barge.

ALISON. You think I'm fat. I'm not fat.

SARAH. No, you're not fat. You even look good pregnant, damn you. But that doesn't help me out much, does it?

ALISON. I miss Rhys.

SARAH. Well, you're married to his father now, and maybe he'd be a somewhat less disoriented person if you'd be so kind as to actually sleep in the same room with him at least once in your life.

ALISON. Since when is it any of your business where I sleep?

SARAH. Don't you get all high and mighty with me, mistress of the manor, or I'll just pack up and get myself out of this place once and for all. Then see where you'd be.

ALISON. Oh, for God's sake, if you want to leave, why the hell don't you just leave? I'm getting so sick of hearing you threaten to every five minutes, at this point I'd be damned happy to get rid of you.

SARAH. And who would take care of poor Mr. Rose if I did go? He'd starve to death. You'd both starve to death. You'd probably eat him.

ALISON. Don't waste any time worrying about me, Sarah.

SARAH. I'm not worried about you. I'm worried about Rhys's innocent child inside you.

ALISON. It doesn't belong to Rhys or you or anybody else. It belongs to me. Nobody else, just me.

SARAH. Then see that you take good care of it. And come help me look for your husband. Oh, never mind. I'll do it myself. You stay here and eat the dog. God, everybody around here is children but me.

(SARAH goes out. ALISON sits down, pulls a carrot out of her pocket, and begins eating it.)

Scene 20

(GAVIN walking by the pond, accompanied by BEL's ghost, in her white dress.)

GAVIN. I should have drained this damned pond years ago. It's full of ghosts. No offense.

BEL. I've grown quite fond of ghosts since I've been dead. I like having them around to gossip with. Just the other day I was having a very interesting conversation with your grandmother Eva, the one who wrote all the demented poems and hid them all over the house. Lord, she's even battier than I was. I like her a lot. Don't you want me talking to you?

GAVIN. Sometimes I wonder if perhaps you'd be happier if you were off doing—I don't know, whatever dead people do.

BEL. I think this is what dead people do—haunt the people who killed us, or loved us—usually it's the same people. What do you expect me to do? Go bowling? You seem to enjoy playing chess with the ghost of your father.

GAVIN. I was hoping I could beat him once in a while, now that he's dead, but he always wins.

BEL. The dead always win. Once you've given up everything, you're invincible.

GAVIN. Also, it scares me that I can't seem to stay away from this pond. I don't like being persistently drawn back to the place where members of my family have traditionally gone to drown themselves.

BEL. Yes, you people are like a bunch of lemmings. I've never understood that.

GAVIN. You died in this pond, too.

BEL. Yes, but I set myself on fire first and jumped out the window. I get my creativity from my Daddy.

GAVIN. Your Daddy was a raving madman.

BEL. Yes, but don't let that discourage you, Gavin. You're getting there. You keep working at it and you'll be just like him.

GAVIN. My father walked into this pond, like his wife and sister before him. Now the distinctions between him and me are becoming more and more blurred in my mind. I walk in the evening in the garden like my father and my grandfather, and see what they saw, and the terror comes from the realization of the terrible circularity of things, the repetition of the figure in the carpet, and the uncertainty of choices made each passing moment when seen in the light of that ultimate certainty of which one does not wish to speak. Time is two complimentary kinds of horror, the real and the imagined, but they're faces of the same dark, monstrous creature. I will never win this game of chess.

BEL. Maybe when you're dead.

GAVIN. I've lost my son.

BEL. Rhys is lucky to be gone from here, and he can take care of himself. I don't think it's Rhys that's really bothering you.

GAVIN. It's you then. I'm grieving over you.

BEL. No, I don't think so. I mean, I'm right here, aren't I? No, there's something else at the core of your grief. And you know what it is.

GAVIN. I have no idea what you're talking about. But then, I never did.

BEL. It's your new wife.

GAVIN. What about her?

BEL. You want her. You desire her. You can't stop thinking about her.

GAVIN. For God's sake, Bel. The girl is my sister.

BEL. That's never stopped anybody in your family before. Your father loved his sister. She told me so herself, only the other day. And after she drowned herself in the pond, he fell in love with that horrible Morgan girl, who was also his sister. You people are pathological that way.

GAVIN. Half-sisters. They were both his half-sisters. He was hardly more than a child when the first happened. She was older. It was her doing. And the second one he was involved with before he knew who she was. It wasn't his fault. Alison is the daughter of both my parents, and I'm fully aware of who she is, and old enough to know better. To think about her in that way would be inexcusable.

BEL. So you married her.

GAVIN. I have never touched her. Never.

BEL. But you've wanted to, very badly, and frankly, Gavin, especially here among the dead, it's more or less the same thing. And her carrying around your son's child, too. Lord, this one will probably have three heads. And also, my love, you fear, in your heart, that she actually did plan all of this, that she meant for this to happen, and still you desire her.

GAVIN. I believe her to be more or less innocent. I believe her involvement with my son was an accident, that she was attempting to comfort him in his grief and things got out of hand. But I see the patterns, the terrible, recurring patterns, and I am horrified. I want to retreat into the mirror. Do you hate me for these things?

BEL. I remember the first time I took off my clothes for you. You married me out of pity, and that impulse to punish yourself for being the bastard son of a half-brother and sister, but when you saw my delicate breasts, the girlish nipples of my breasts, and put your mouth to them, you forgot everything. At least until she came. Admit it. Admit that you desire her.

GAVIN. I DO NOT DESIRE HER.

(He turns. SARAH is standing there.)

SARAH. And just who are we talking to now? The Holy Ghost?
GAVIN. My wife.
SARAH. Your wife is in the house, eating everything that's not nailed down.
GAVIN. My first wife.
SARAH. Your first wife is dead.
GAVIN. I'm aware of that.
SARAH. Well, I hope she makes more sense now than when she was alive. Why don't you come in the house? It's getting cold out here.
GAVIN. Time folds back on itself. When I was a boy, I looked out that gable window and saw my grandfather wandering out here, talking to himself, and my father trying to persuade him to come inside. I remember thinking what a poor, crazy old man he was, and how frightening, although he was always kind enough to me. Now here I am, not nearly as old but perhaps more crazy, and you're trying to coax me into the house. Things come round to get you, you find yourself taking over the roles of the old people you took for granted as a child, and whatever you've had contempt for in your cruel and stupid youth, that's what you turn into when you're old. Why don't you go and marry Evan Unkefer?
SARAH. Evan Unkefer can wait.
GAVIN. Not forever he can't. We have a finite number of opportunities in this world, Sarah, and we let them get by us, one by one, waiting for something better to come along, and then wake up one day as if from a dream and find ourselves old, deformed, lost, our hands gnarled like the roots of trees, and nobody has any use for us.
SARAH. You're forty-two, and you talk like you're Methuselah.
GAVIN. Don't wait too long, Sarah.

SARAH. You mean I should marry the first person I stumble across, like you did?

GAVIN. I could have done worse.

SARAH. I don't see how.

GAVIN. You were very fond of Bel.

SARAH. Yes, I was, but I never would have been stupid enough to marry her.

GAVIN. When she died, I should have married you.

SARAH. Me? Married me? What makes you think I'd have had you?

GAVIN. Yes. You'd have put me off until something better came along, and perhaps for you something will, but don't wait too long and get trapped here. Perhaps you're trapped already.

SARAH. I'm not trapped anywhere. I'm a free person, and I'll do exactly what I please.

GAVIN. Just don't wait for Rhys forever.

SARAH. I'm not waiting for anybody. Now, come in the house and stop talking nonsense.

GAVIN. I just want to watch the sun go down, me and the crows. Then I'll go in, I promise. I'll watch the sunset, and then I'll go in.

SARAH. Well. All right. I guess there's no harm in that.

GAVIN. There have been times, you know, Sarah, when I really think you're all that's held us together.

SARAH. I'm not sure anything's holding you together.

GAVIN. There are points in the history of a family, over time, when the line could easily flicker and go out, when it hangs by the mortal flesh of one small child. You must make sure nothing happens to Alison's child.

SARAH. I'm sure plenty will happen to him, and you and I will watch out for him together, now come inside and have some supper. I don't like the looks of those crows. I've never entirely trusted crows. I don't know what exactly I expect them to do, but I don't like them. You'll come right in?

GAVIN. Yes. Very soon. *(She looks at him, hesitates, then goes.)* Crows and owls. This place is full of crows and owls. *(Pause.)* Something is happening inside my head. Something is happening. How curious. The house in the woods.

BEL. Gavin, you know, it's rather lonely, being dead. I wish you'd come and join me.

GAVIN. *(As the darkness slowly begins to close in on him.)* The house in the woods, in the war, the grail house, was this house all along. The labyrinth is the inside of my brain. All of them live in it, Rudd and Merlin and my father, my mother, poor drowned Jenny and my grandfather Zach, crazy Eva the mad poetess, old Jake Armitage and batty old Margaret. I can see back through time and forward, Matt's children, Alison's children, grief, a brother and a sister, Davey old in the garden. They will drain the pond when I am dead but the ghosts will remain and I will be one of them, and this thing which is happening inside my head like a series of explosions of light and I am in this other place, like the stage of a theatre, the house is dark and I hear these voices, there is a performance going on, and the performance is my life, in interlocking plays, and the lives of all those who have bred me, and all those I will breed, dramatis personae, lurking in the water, and a naked girl at the window, beckoning me, so lovely, and then—

BEL. *(From the darkness that surrounds him.)* Gavin?
GAVIN. Yes?
BEL. You won't leave me any more now.
GAVIN. No. I won't leave you now.
BEL. Never?
GAVIN. Never.

(GAVIN walks out of the light and towards her, towards the pond, into the darkness, and disappears. The sound of crows.)

Scene 21

(MATT in his office. ALISON in the parlor.)

MATT. Sarah found him in the water, not far out. Doc said he was dead before he went under, probably a stroke caused by a blood clot. We made sure there was no official mention of the fight with Rhys. And of course, as always, I was there to help.

(MATT has moved into the parlor with ALISON. SARAH comes in from the front door.)

SARAH. That's the last of them. I thought they'd never leave.
ALISON. It wasn't really very many.
SARAH. The same as came for her. I'm surprised it was that many. Most people won't even come out here. Half of what people do is lust or fear, and the rest is morbid curiosity. I'd better wrap up some of this food. I don't understand why when somebody dies, everybody brings food. Are we supposed to eat our way out of mourning, or what? Nobody is hungry who really gave a damn. Most of it goes to waste. It's a metaphor for life. That's all right. Don't offer to help. It's an excuse not to think.

(SARAH goes into the kitchen. MATT looks at ALISON.)

MATT. Are you all right?
ALISON. You've been very good through all this, Matt. I've always known, all of my life, that whenever I was in trouble, you'd be there, no matter what. It means a lot to me. You mean a lot to me.
MATT. You don't have to say these things. I have no plans to make any trouble for you.
ALISON. You think I didn't mean that?

MATT. It doesn't matter what you mean. It's done now.

ALISON. You think I'm the cause of all this. You hate me. It isn't my fault. I didn't mean for any of this to happen.

MATT. Whatever you did or didn't mean to happen, it all goes back to way before you, before anybody alive now. We're just playing out the game. I don't hate you. Sometimes I wish to God I did. *(Pause.)* Is there anything else I can do tonight?

ALISON. No.

MATT. Are you two going to be all right alone here?

ALISON. We're fine.

MATT. I'll come by in the morning. There are papers to sign, but essentially he left everything equally to you and Rhys, and he set aside money for Sarah and your sister. I'm to manage things for you.

ALISON. Fine.

MATT. So, I'll see you tomorrow.

ALISON. Yes.

MATT. I'll keep trying to get in touch with Rhys. I'm sure if he'd had any idea, he'd be here.

ALISON. I know.

MATT. Do you want me to stay over tonight?

ALISON. No. You go home and be with your wife. We'll see you tomorrow.

MATT. All right. Say good night to Sarah for me.

ALISON. I will.

MATT. Good night.

ALISON. Good night.

(MATT looks at her. He hesitates. Then goes. SARAH returns.)

SARAH. I wrapped up some food for him to take. Is he gone?

ALISON. He'll be back in the morning.

SARAH. That's when I'll be leaving. Don't look at me like that. This time I actually mean it. I've buried the last of them. Now I'm getting out of here before somebody buries me.

ALISON. Sarah, you can't leave me all alone here.

SARAH. I'd think you'd be glad to get rid of me.

ALISON. I can't be all alone in this big old house with a baby coming.

SARAH. You won't be alone for long. When Rhys finds out, he'll come back.

ALISON. I don't think he will.

SARAH. He will, sooner or later.

ALISON. I need you, Sarah.

SARAH. Matt will look out for you. He's still crazy in love with you.

ALISON. Matt can't be coming out here all the time. He's got a wife and child to take care of.

SARAH. Don't worry. The wife has consumption. She won't last forever. Then maybe you can have them both, Matt and Rhys. You'd like that, wouldn't you?

ALISON. Sarah, I've just buried my husband.

SARAH. Yes, I'm sure you're very broken up about it. You just knew the man long enough to kill his wife, get pregnant by his son, trick him into marrying you, drive him crazy, get him killed, and take over everything. Well, now you've got it all. I hope it makes you happy.

ALISON. Even if you believe all that about me, what about the baby?

SARAH. You can pay somebody else to tend to that.

ALISON. I don't want somebody else. I want you.

SARAH. Why the hell would you want me?

ALISON. Because you're the only friend I've got in the world.

SARAH. I'm not your friend. Matt Armitage is your friend.

ALISON. Matt Armitage is a married man who's in love with me. You're my friend.

SARAH. Will you stop saying that? I am not your friend. I don't

want to be your damned friend.
ALISON. Are you Rhys's friend? Are you his child's friend?

(Pause.)

SARAH. I'm making hot chocolate before I go to bed. Do you want some?
ALISON. Will you stay with me? Please?

(Pause.)

SARAH. For the child. Only for the child.
ALISON. Thank you.
SARAH. We'll both live to regret it. *(Pause.)* It's cold in here. I'll warm the milk.

(SARAH goes back into the kitchen.)

MATT. *(In his office, drinking.)* Love is the only poison that matters.
ALISON. My house.
MATT. In the ancient romances of Europe, the roses intertwine above the gravestones. It's a dangerous beauty. It makes you bleed, and it grows like a labyrinth.
ALISON. I am here in my house. My mother's house.
MATT. Sorrow and guilt woven so deep into the fabric of desire that nothing can separate them out.
ALISON. I've done what I was raised to do.
MATT. Generation upon generation we devour one another in the holy naked communion of the damned.
ALISON. I've destroyed them, one by one, and gotten your house back for you.
MATT. When I close my eyes I see a young girl grieving in the

rain, for her future and her past, for what made her and for what she is about to make, gazing at the massive old labyrinth of house in dark Ohio woods, all past and future contained within it, desire and hate, all things come round again.

ALISON. I hate this place.

MATT. And now I have the great privilege of going home to my wife, my tender, fragile wife. To hold my wife in my arms. My wife, who loves me very much.

ALISON. I hate it.

MATT. Who loves me very much.

(MATT finishes his drink, then goes.)

ALISON. *(Sitting alone on the sofa in the parlor, as the light begins to close in on her.)* This is my prison. This is the prison of granted wishes. I have written out the story of my life, and now I am trapped here, my child is trapped inside my body, and I am trapped inside this house, and this house is trapped in the wicked mind of God, and I will be trapped in this evil place until the day I die. And no doubt after that as well.

(She sits on the sofa, one hand on her stomach, alone and unhappy. Sound of ticking clocks. The light fades on her and goes out. Darkness.)

THE END

NOTEBOOK: TRISTAN

1

Thales said all things are full of gods. Heraclitus believed that the universe of change is generated by the constant interplay of opposites, flowing like a river. You can't step into the same river twice, for the river is constantly changing. The union of all opposites is in the Logos, the word. What he is describing, I think, is irony, the seed of a thing's opposite locked inside itself, which is what an actor must find to play a character, a playwright to write a play. The Logos is what John speaks of at the beginning of his gospel: In the beginning was the Word, and the Word was with God, and the Word was God. This is pantheism of a sort, the world being a forest of symbols, everything charged with meaning, as in Baudelaire. We know this as children, then are required to forget it as the price for being admitted into the society of adults. If we do not forget it, we are judged lunatics, or we become writers, or both.

The world appears to be hopelessly fragmented, but in fact everything is connected to everything else. To observe is to make a distinction, to cut a boundary between the self and what is observed, but it is also, paradoxically, to unite all observed events in the labyrinth of the brain of the observer. The labyrinth is a powerful symbol of the basic interconnectedness of all things, but also of the bewildering nature of our journey through time. The fact that on the other side of the wall of any corridor of the labyrinth might be the one I love, very close, but that I must travel through a long, complex and tortuous nightmare of tunnels to get to her--this is for me the most powerful objective correlative of the artist's investigation into truth, which is always, on some level, also the soul's search for love. If one could fly over the labyrinth like Daedalus one could put aside the powerful illusion of fragmentation and see that the labyrinth is one complex organism--for the labyrinth is in fact alive. It is the inside of our brains. The dark old house, the rooms and corridors, the dark forest of Grimm, these are other faces of the labyrinth, the endless library of Babel, the city of infinite pathways, the labyrinth of the brain.

2

To vagueness there are no boundaries. Anything could mean anything. With ambiguity there are boundaries, but we are not sure where to draw them. Vagueness presents an infinite number of choices. In ambiguity, the number of choices is finite, but we don't know the number. There are no maps to vagueness. With ambiguity, there are maps, but the maps are drawn differently as we perceive things differently, understand things in different ways, collect different pieces of the puzzle. The symbol is the basic unit of art, and the symbol is an embodiment of ambiguity. Irony, uncertainty, and passion. Out of this I make worlds.

3

A play told in a prism, each of the characters sees the story from a certain point of view, cares about some elements of it more than others. We see the story reflected through them turn and turn about. The Pendragon house in the years 1887-88 is the center of their universe, but the tendrils of their agony reach far back into the past and far into their future. Sarah is a servant, she is cast as a minor character in the play of their lives, but she is the glue that holds their world together, at times almost single-handedly. Bel is insane, but she can see some things much more clearly than the others, especially after she is dead. Alison is sent to destroy the people and regain the house, but she comes to love the people she is destroying, and to hate the house that is her inheritance. Matt is loyal to his wife but cannot help betraying her in his heart. Rhys, who was to be the inheritor, renounces his inheritance and is for the rest of his life a journalist with no home. Gavin, who has never felt a part of the Pendragons, becomes one of them by dying like them. He comes to understand that the labyrinth is inside his brain, not outside, or rather that what appears to be outside is really the objective correlative of what is inside him, has always been, and the Grail House he saw in the woods long ago is the Pendragon house itself, seen through a different pair of spectacles.

4

In the cycle of Pendragon plays, Gavin and Bel also appear in *Fisher King* and *Sorceress*, and Gavin is in *Green Man* as well. Matt, Alison, Rhys and Sarah all appear in *Chronicles*, and the latter three also in *Dramatis Personae*. Rhys is the protagonist of *Pendragon,* and Alison also appears in *The Circus Animals' Desertion*. Time is a labyrinth of interconnected plays and interconnected lives. Their dates of birth and death are as follows:

Gavin Rose (1846-1888)
Bel Rhys Rose (1847-1887)
Matthew Armitage (1850-1921)
Alison Morgan Rose Armitage (1868-1946)
John Rhys Pendragon Rose (1870-1949)
Sarah Pritchard (1870-1950).

When *Tristan* begins, in 1887, Matt's little boy David Armitage is 7, his wife Mary Elizabeth Scott Armitage is 27, and Alison's sister, Holly Robey, back in Maryland, is 39. Margaret Cornish had died in 1879, Jacob Armitage in 1874. As Tristan meets another Iseult, so Rhys, who will drop his last name and become the journalist John Rhys Pendragon, will find another Alison in that unlikeliest of places, Boise, Idaho, the story of which is told in *Pendragon*. Rhys will later return to Armitage long enough to father another child on Alison (their children will be the doomed lovers John Rose and Jessie Armitage of *Laestrygonians*), and will meet Alison McPherson in Boise in 1910. At Christmas in 1920 Rhys will once again return to Armitage (in *Chronicles)*, in mourning for his dead wife and estranged from her little girl, and try to settle things with Matt and Alison before Matt dies. He will return for the last time in 1946 (in *Dramatis Personae)*, when Alison is dying.

5

Gavin reads Malory in his father's study, hoping to somehow there unravel the secrets of the Pendragons. All of them find, from time to time, the mad poems of Eva Pendragon hidden around the house, in books, in furniture, behind pictures, in old drawers. Past, present and future are a woven tapestry in the labyrinth of the house and the labyrinth of plays. You can step into the labyrinth at any point and be at its center. Wherever you enter it, that is the beginning. The path through the labyrinth may lead you from any play to any other play. Each play is a separate and totally self-sufficient universe unto itself, but each play is also linked to each other play. My life's work is a labyrinth.

6

Fay has taught Alison to play chess. Holly never liked it, but Alison took to it immediately. She would play chess with Matt when he'd come to visit at Mary's Grove. At the Pendragon house, she plays chess with Rhys. Sarah thinks it's a stupid game. Alison wins at chess but loses Rhys. As a boy, he spends much time in the woods. He also reads voraciously, and wants to travel. When he leaves home to write for the newspapers, he will drop his last name and thus separate himself from his father. Tristan changed his name to Tantris, but could not escape his fate thereby. The hawks circle always. They are an image of the danger that surrounds them all, constantly following them. The love potion is the wine that Rhys gives Alison the first night she comes to the house. Gavin also drinks some. Sarah is like Brangane—she would like to take Alison's place. The mythology fragments and turns into its ironic counterpoint. In fact, it is Alison who takes Sarah's place in the affections of Rhys. There is a huge old tree on the Pendragon property, with CR (Christopher Rumpley) carved into it. This tree will endure to the end of the cycle. She dreams of blood-spattered flour around her bed. Sarah makes bread. Alison loves the dawn. Years later, she will die at dawn. Sarah is a moon goddess, but perhaps not always, in the end, a chaste one.

7
Heidegger says that the roots of the past lie in the future. Kierkegaard says that life can only be understood backwards, but must be lived forwards. Plays are just like this.

8
Gavin has from birth been aware that he lives in a world where there are complex secrets involving his own identity, but the silence of his father has helped to mold in him a strong feeling that these mysteries must not be spoken of, let alone uncovered. The result is that at critical times in his life he has turned away from the opportunity to know things—as in his experience with the Grail House in the war (in *Fisher King*). And even when he is attempting to investigate and understand, as in his experience in Mary's Grove (in *Green Man*), the investigation leads to disaster, death, and a terrible feeling of guilt, and he is driven more deeply into his shell of non-investigation. Rhys is the opposite. His profession becomes a constant investigation into truth. But in another way, he is using his investigation to run away from his own heritage.

9
I cherish the illusion of home. When the illusion of love can no longer be sustained, the illusion that one is safely clasped in the arms of one's own personal labyrinth can provide a powerful counterfeit of peace. The only genuine currency of peace, of course, is death, but that is what we save. We do not want to spend that until the end is forced upon us by the sheer mortal contingency of flesh and blood decaying. Home is a practice coffin. Sleep is a rehearsal for death. Dreams are the fragments from which we fashion art. Art is what we do while we're waiting.

ABOUT THE AUTHOR

Don Nigro has written over 200 plays, 102 of which are published by Samuel French in 32 volumes (see listings on pages 133—136). His work has been produced in all fifty states, in London, Oxford, Edinburgh, Glasgow, Munich, Freiburg, Vienna, Budapest, Bombay, Calcutta, Madras, Hong Kong and Mexico City and in Canada, Switzerland, Iceland, Australia, Japan, South Africa, the Virgin Islands and Bermuda. He has won grants from the National Endowment for the Arts (for *Fisher King*), the Mary Robert Rinehart Foundation (for *Terre Haute*), and the Ohio Arts Council, has twice been a finalist for the National Repertory Theatre Foundation's National Play Award (for *Anima Mundi* and *The Dark Sonnets of the Lady*), and twice been James Thurber Writer in Residence at Thurber House in Columbus. His work has been translated into Italian, German, Russian, Spanish and Polish.